foundations for faith

The Basics for Knowing God

Neighborhood Bible Studies Publishers
Dobbs Ferry, New York

The Basics for Knowing God

9 Discussions for Group Bible Study
Virginia Bowen and Lorraine Fleischman

Scripture quotations, unless otherwise indicated, are taken from the HOLY BIBLE, NEW INTERNATIONAL VERSION®. Copyright © 1973, 1978, 1984 by International Bible Society. Used by permission of Zondervan Publishing House. All rights reserved.

All rights reserved. No part of this book may be reproduced or transmitted in any form or by any means, electronic or mechanical, including photocopying, recording, or any information storage and retrieval system without written permission from Neighborhood Bible Studies, 56 Main Street, Dobbs Ferry, New York, 10522.

Copyright© 1987, 1999 by Virginia Bowen and Lorraine Fleischman

ISBN 1-880266-33-4
First Printing 1999
Printed in the United States of America
Cover by Tom Greene

CONTENTS

How to Use this Study Guide 7

Introduction 13

Discussion 1 **Genesis 1**
What is God Like According to the Bible? ... 15

Discussion 2 **Psalm 139**
How Does God Relate to the People He Created? 21

Discussion 3 **Genesis 2**
What Provisions Does God Make for Humankind? 25

Discussion 4 **Genesis 3**
What Changed God's Good World? 29

Discussion 5 **Romans 1:18-32**
How Did the Trouble Spread? 35

Discussion 6 **The Gospels**
What Did God Do About the Problem? 39

Discussion 7 **The Gospels**
Did Jesus Really Come Back from the Dead? 45

Discussion 8 **Mark, Isaiah, New Testament Letters**
Why Did Jesus Have to Die? 49

Discussion 9 *The Point of It All* 53

What Should Our Group Study Next? 61

HOW TO USE THIS STUDY GUIDE

The steps people take to a living relationship with God are unique to each individual. However, it is necessary for everyone to consider *certain basic issues* dealt with in these studies. The studies do not assume previous Bible knowledge.

Two reasons for *not* knowing God are a lack of information, and a resistant attitude toward God. These nine studies provide information about God, about ourselves, and about how God wants us to respond to him. Each study includes suggestions to help people respond to God at the level of their understanding at that time.

HELPS FOR GROUP PARTICIPATION

Why Questions?

This study guide helps people discover for themselves what the Bible says. People remember best what they discover and what they express in their own words, rather than by only listening to what someone else says. The study guide provides three kinds of questions:

> *What does the Bible say? What are the facts?*
> *What is the meaning of these facts?*
> *How does this passage apply to my life?*

Observe the facts carefully before you *interpret* the meaning of your observations. Then *apply* the truths you have discovered to life today. Resist the temptation to skip the fact questions. Find the facts quickly so you can spend more time on their meaning and application. The questions in these studies require simple, obvious answers, not deep complicated ones.

Preparation

Everyone reads the Bible passages during the week in preparation for the discussion. If any members of the group are absent, try to study that discussion with them before the next session so they will understand what follows.

Maximize Participation

- Encourage each member to take a turn being the question-asker for a discussion.
- Ask for volunteers to read the Bible passages.
- Share responsibility for the meeting place and for any refreshments.

Tools for an Effective Study

1. A contemporary translation of the Bible such as:

    New International Version (NIV)
    New Living Translation (NLT)
    Contemporary English Version (CEV)
    Jerusalem Bible (JB)
    New Revised Standard Version (NRSV)

2. A study guide for each person in the group.

3. A standard dictionary.

Guidelines for Effective Study

1. Stay with the passage under discussion.

2. Avoid tangents. If the subject is not addressed in the passage, wait to discuss it until after the study.

3. Let the Bible speak for itself. Don't quote other authorities or rewrite it to say what you want it to say.

4. Apply the passage personally and honestly.

5. Listen to one another to sharpen your insights.

6. Prepare by reading the Bible passage and thinking about the questions during the week.

HELPS FOR THE QUESTION-ASKER

1. Prepare by reading the passage several times, using different versions if possible. Ask God's help to understand it. Consider how the questions might be answered. Observe which questions can be answered quickly, and which may require more time.

2. Begin on time.

3. Lead the group in opening prayer, which you may write out if you wish. Or, ask someone ahead of time to pray. Don't take anyone by surprise.

4. Ask for a different volunteer to read each Bible section. Read the study question. Wait for an answer. Rephrase the question if necessary. Skip questions already answered by the discussion. Resist the temptation to answer the question yourself.

5. Encourage everyone to participate. Ask the group, "What do the rest of you think?" "What else could be added?"

6. Receive all answers warmly. If needed, ask, "In which verse did you find that?" "How does that fit with verse...?"

7. If a tangent arises ask, "Do we find the answer to that here?" Or suggest, "Let's write that down and look for the information as we go along."

8. Discourage members who are too talkative by saying, "When I read the next question, let's hear from someone who hasn't spoken yet today."

9. Bring the study to a conclusion on time.

Other Points to Keep in Mind

1. Be prepared to lend a Bible for the duration of the series to anyone without one. *Use a contemporary version.* For Bible study, standard translations are preferable to a paraphrase.

2. As people study the Bible for the first time, they need to *see the major points of each study*. Avoid detailed explanations confusing to a newcomer.

3. Encourage people to *see what the Bible says*, whether or not they agree with it.

4. *Avoid detailed discussion of side issues.* Suggest that those interested talk about any such issues after the session is finished.

FOR THE PERSON INITIATING A STUDY

Before You Start

1. Before speaking to others about this study series, read and think through the nine studies as if you were hearing it all for the first time.

2. It is helpful to find someone with whom to share in prayer, and in facilitating the group.

3. Ask God to lead you to people he has prepared, for whom this study series will be meaningful and helpful.

As You Begin to Invite People

1. Be alert to remarks and attitudes which show that individuals are thinking about spiritual issues, are having problems, or are sensing a need.

2. Ask questions to find interested people:
   Have you read the Bible as an adult?
   Do you think that God exists?
   What do you think God is like?
   Did you ever wish you could know God?

3. Invite people to discover what the Bible says about such questions as:
   What is God like?
   How does God relate to people?
   If God is powerful and good, why is the world in the condition it is today?
   How can we know God?

4. To stimulate interest, you could use some of the discussion titles to describe the series briefly. Then say, "This study series puts it all together—what the Bible says God is like and how we can know God. While there is no pressure to believe anything, the series is a frank examination of what the Bible says."

5. If people seem hesitant about a nine-session series, suggest that they come the first two times to see what it is like.

Who

One or two Christians familiar with the Bible can use these studies with two to four people new to the Bible. A group of four to six people gives participants the opportunity to talk about the questions, doubts and insights that individuals may have.

One to One

These studies can also be used one-to-one in a "study together" atmosphere, not as teacher/pupil. Take turns reading aloud the Bible passages. Allow the newcomer time to think and usually to answer the discussion questions first. Keep to simple basics.

Where, What and When

- Meet in a home if possible.
- Rotate homes if convenient, or use a meeting room in a neutral location comfortable for new people.
- There are nine study sessions lasting about one hour each.
- Meeting once a week allows individuals time to read and prepare the Bible sections being studied.
- Since each study builds on the previous discussions, it is better *not* to add people to the group *after Discussion 1*. Encourage interested latecomers to begin when the series is repeated.
- Those who wish to write out answers to questions in their study preparation should do this in a separate notebook. During the discussion time, people will benefit more if they listen and talk, rather than trying to record answers.

WHAT NEXT?

During these studies many people become so interested in the Bible that they want to continue further study. A biography of Jesus Christ is the next appropriate step. The *Gospel of Mark* is the shortest of the four accounts of Jesus' life, moves the quickest and has fewest Old Testament references. (However, if your group includes members from Jewish or Muslim religious backgrounds, you may wish to begin with the *Gospel of Matthew*.)

If you would like to continue your study together, Neighborhood Bible Studies guides can be ordered from the NBS office 1-800-369-0307. Plan to order enough study guides so that each member of the group has his or her own copy. For additional help in establishing a healthy group, order for the group one copy of the handbook, *How to Start a Neighborhood Bible Study*. For a full listing of NBS guides, see page 63.

INTRODUCTION

The Bible is a library of books whose central theme is the relationship between the Creator of the universe and humankind. Many people have questions like:

How did this world and its inhabitants come to be?

If an all-powerful God exists, why is the world today in such a deplorable state?

Does God really care for us?

Is it possible to know God?

The studies in *Foundations for Faith* explore these questions and help to develop a basic framework of Bible knowledge.

Some Bible sections are not studied in chronological order, but in the order in which many people's questions can be handled more effectively. Since this is an introductory series, each discussion deals with only one or two major concepts. For people new to Bible study, Bible references can be understood as follows:

Genesis 1:1-5; 2:1-3 refers to: the book of Genesis, chapter 1, verses 1 to 5; chapter 2, verses 1 to 3.

Isaiah 52:13—53:12 refers to: the book of Isaiah, chapter 52, verse 13 through chapter 53, verse 12.

Foundations for Faith

DISCUSSION 1

What is God Like According to the Bible?

What do you think of when you see or hear the word *God*? Share your ideas for a few minutes.

There are many ideas about *God,* and many religions in the world. How can we know which one is true? Or will any of them do?

We can't see, hear or touch God. Unless God reveals himself to us, we cannot know anything about God with certainty. Has God ever revealed himself? The purpose of these studies is to see what the Bible says about God and how we can know God. After carefully and honestly examining what the Bible says, each person will be better able to choose how he or she will respond to God. In this first study we begin to see what the Bible says God is like.

Read Genesis 1:1—2:3, looking for all you can learn about what God is like.

In the Beginning
Genesis 1:1-5

1. What words describe God's actions in verses 1-5?

2. What would God have to be like in order to do these things?

Genesis 1:6—2:3

3. What was the method by which God created (verses 3, 6, 9, 11, 14, 20, 24)?

4. In order to accomplish all this, what would God have to be like?

5. What does this section tell us about God's relationship to nature?

6. Observe the order in which God creates things in the six days.

    What do you learn about God from this?

*Note: The Hebrew word for **day** can refer to the hours of daylight, a twenty-four hour day, or an indefinite period of time. If an indefinite period of time is meant here, the length of each day may have been different, some even long ages. The Bible is not written as a science textbook explaining details of the origin of the universe. While there are differing opinions about the actual events and time frame of creation, the Bible clearly states that God brought everything into existence.*

7. What does God think of each thing he makes (verses 4, 10, 12, 18, 21, 25)?

How does this compare with most things we make?

8. What is created on the sixth day?

   What do humans and animals have in common, according to verses 24-30?

9. What distinctions are made between humans and animals?

   How are human beings different from everything else God has created?

10. In what ways do you see that human beings express the image of God as God is portrayed in this first chapter of Genesis?

11. In what ways is God greater than humans?

    How does it affect your understanding of God when you see that the Bible says a human being is like God, not that God is like a human being?

12. What order does God establish in the relationship of humans to the rest of creation (verses 26, 28)?

13. What difference would it make in your life if you believed that you are made in the image of the God presented in this passage?

14. God *blessed* (verses 22, 28) and *gave* (verses 29, 30). What do these actions reveal about God?

    What is God's final assessment of what he has made (verse 31)?

Summary

1. Recall the actions of God in Genesis 1:1—2:3. How would you describe God from these verses?

2. What do the words *in the beginning* tell you about God, God's existence, and God's relationship to time as we know it?

3. How is the God revealed in the Bible different from some people's ideas about "god", such as:

    "Nature"—the sun, moon, etc. are gods. There are myriads of gods.

    God is a dispenser of divine favors upon request, to use when you need help, but who can be ignored at other times.

    God is a product of our minds: if you believe God exists, he does; if you don't believe he exists, he doesn't.

4. In Genesis, God is described not as a created being, but as the source of all life, a living person who made all things including the first human beings. What attitudes do you think are appropriate for people to have toward such a God?

    How do you feel about the idea that God rather than humankind is central in the universe?

5. What questions about God has this study prompted for you? If you wish, write your questions here in this study guide. Perhaps the following studies will begin to answer some of these questions.

The Bible begins with the assumption that God is eternal, and that God created the universe out of nothing by his power and design. Our abilities to plan, choose, evaluate, communicate, take responsibility, and act creatively—all express how we are in the image of God.

In preparation for the next study:

How does this all-powerful Creator want to relate to us today? Has God gone off and left the world to run on its own? Or does God want to be involved in our lives today?

As you think about these questions, study Psalm 139 before the next meeting, using the questions provided for Discussion 2.

Foundations for Faith

DISCUSSION 2

How Does God Relate to the People He Created?

In Chapter One of Genesis, we discovered that God created man and woman similar to himself. Does this all-powerful Creator want to relate to us today? Has he gone off and left the world to run on its own, or does God want to be involved in our lives?

In most religions, people are seeking God or seeking "something." According to the Bible, *God is seeking people*. In this Psalm the poet David recognizes God's intimate involvement in his life.

Read Psalm 139:1-6. As one person reads this section aloud, listen for what God knows about each of us.

1. According to these verses, what specific things does God know about us?

    How much of our lives does this include?

2. What contact is there between the writer David and God who knows so much about him (verse 5)?

    For what different reasons may you put your hand on someone?

How do you feel when somebody suddenly puts a hand on your shoulder?

Read Psalm 139:7-12. As one person reads aloud, put yourself in the psalm-writer's place, sensing how he feels.

3. What questions come to David's mind (verse 7)?

   What thoughts and feelings might prompt him to ask such questions?

4. What possible places to flee does David consider?

   Why would any such attempts to escape from God be futile?

5. What are some of the ways we try to escape from God today?

6. What do you learn about God's attitude toward us from his actions in verses 1, 5, 10?

   Why would it be difficult for God to lead a person who is running away from him?

Read Psalm 139:13-18, sensing the writer's feelings.

7. What other things does the psalm-writer realize that God knows about him?

   To what extent has God been involved in David's life?

   What does this tell you about God?

8. How does David react to this realization (verses 14, 17, 18)?

   What is your reaction to the idea that God thinks about you, and knows you so completely?

Read Psalm 139:19-22, looking for some people's attitudes toward God.

9. How does the psalm-writer describe the people who hate God?

10. Why, do you think, would people choose to hate God?

Read Psalm 139:23, 24, sensing how the writer feels about God now.

11. What does David now ask God to do for him?

12. How are these requests different from David's previous thoughts about fleeing from God?

    What do you think has made this change in him?

13. Since God already knows everything about him (verses 1-4), why do you think that David asks God to *know* him and *search* him even more?

14. We may come to the same reactions as the psalm-writer—try to run away from God, or marvel at his knowledge and ask him to lead us. You may want to ask God to lead you as the writer does in verses 23, 24. Take a few moments now in silence to tell God whatever you are thinking.

Summary

According to the Bible, God the Creator is all-powerful, all-knowing and present everywhere. God also cares about us, wants to be intimately involved in our lives, and wants to lead us. We may try to escape from God, or choose to be glad for his knowledge of us and commit ourselves to his searching and leading.

If you wish more information about what God is like, read Psalm 103 and Isaiah 40 during the coming week.

In preparation for the next study:

Read Genesis 2. Into what kind of situation did God, who cares so much for people, place the first man and woman? Study this chapter using the questions provided in Discussion 3.

DISCUSSION 3

What Provisions Does God Make for Humankind?

If you could create a brand new world, what would you consider the perfect ingredients for a beautiful, livable and challenging situation? As you look at Genesis 1:26—2:25, what does God choose as the ideal living situation for the first man and woman?

Read Genesis 2:4-25, noticing the things that are good about the world God created.

1. What additional details do you learn about the creation of man (verse 7)?

   Compare 1:24, 25 and 1:26, 27; 2:7. What value does God seem to place on humankind?

2. If you were painting a picture of the garden in which God puts man, what would you include in it (verses 8-15)?

3. What is the only thing God declares *not good* (verse 18)?

How does naming the animals (verse 20) help the man to see his need, and to appreciate the companion God provides for him (verses 21-23)?

4. From verses 18b, 21-25, what impresses you about the relationship between the man and his wife?

5. God gives the man and woman opportunity to use the capabilities he has given them. What do their responsibilities include (1:26, 28; 2:15, 19, 20)?

   How does what God expects them to do give expression to the image of God in them?

6. Many people today seem to have no relationship with the God who created them, or any consciousness of his being involved in their lives. How does Adam come to be in this beautiful place, to have satisfying work, and to find exactly the right wife (verses 15, 19, 20-22)?

   What does this show you about God and his personal care for human beings?

7. As Creator and Ruler over all, the LORD God delegates responsibilities and sets limits. What opportunities to choose to obey or disobey the LORD God are included in the design of the garden?

   What is the couple free to do, and what may they not do?

8. What would be the consequence of disobeying the LORD God, and when would this happen (verses 16, 17)?

9. Since Adam and his wife live in an ideal situation with all their needs completely supplied, do you think God's command in verse 17 would be easy or difficult for them to obey?

Why?

Note: Although the LORD God influenced and cared for his creation, the situation was not like "fate" with a predetermined outcome. God made humans with minds and wills he expected them to use to rule the earth and its creatures (1:27-30; 2:8, 15).

Summary

1. What does the account tell you about what God is like, his character?

2. What special care does God show for the first man and woman (verses 7-9, 15-17, 18-22)?

3. What impression do you get of the kind of relationship the LORD God wants to have with the human beings he has created in his own image?

In preparation for the next study:

Read carefully Genesis 3. Look for what happens to change the ideal situation that exists in Genesis 2. Use the questions in Discussion 4 to help you in your study.

Foundations for Faith

DISCUSSION 4

What Changed God's Good World?

Do you ever wonder why some things that are so good as they begin end up so bad? Think of an example from your own life or the lives of people you have known. God looked at his creation and saw that it was very good (Genesis 1:31), but our world doesn't fit that description. What happened to that good world? How does the Bible answer this question?

Read Genesis 3:1-6, looking for what changes the harmonious situation of Genesis 2.

1. Describe the serpent who now appears on the scene.

*Note: Revelation 12:9 in the New Testament identifies the serpent as **that ancient serpent called the devil or Satan, who leads the whole world astray.***

2. The serpent begins to tempt by misquoting God. What impression of the LORD God does this misquote give? (Compare 3:1 and 2:16, 17.)

   How does the woman's answer differ from what God said?

3. What does the serpent suggest about God's motives in forbidding the man and woman to eat the fruit from the tree of the knowledge of good and evil (verses 4, 5)?

4. How do the serpent's arguments affect the way the woman looks at the tree and its fruit (verse 6)?

   What motivates the woman to disobey God?

   At this point, what choices does the man face? (Compare verses 5, 6 with 2:16, 17.)

5. When the woman and her husband choose to place their human judgment above God's command and warning, what are they saying about themselves, and about God?

   What does the fact that *each* of them has this choice to obey or disobey, reveal about God the Creator?

Read Genesis 3:7-24, looking for the results of disobedience.

6. What changes in the couple's relationship result from their disobedience to God (2:23-25; 3:7, 12, 13)?

   What change occurs in their relationship with God (verses 8-10)?

7. Disobedience to God introduces blame. Whom besides his wife does Adam blame?

   Whom does the woman blame?

What are some examples of the way we make the same sort of excuses about circumstances in our lives?

8. What happens to the couple's ability to see themselves honestly?

9. The LORD God judges the guilty couple and curses the serpent and the ground. What judgments does God pronounce on each (verses 14-19, 23, 24)?

10. God had said, *"when you eat of it you shall surely die."* In what way do Adam and his wife die when they disobey God?

11. Adam and Eve have already made themselves clothes of fig leaves. Confirming their need for covering, what more adequate provision does God make (verse 21)?

    What dies to give them covering?

    What connection between disobedience and death does God's action suggest?

12. Instead of totally rejecting Adam and Eve for what they have done, how does God show his continued care for them (verses 8-10, 21, 22-24)?

    Who initiates the next contact between God and the couple after they eat the fruit (verses 8-10)?

13. What future hope does God give Adam and Eve (verse 15)?

Since the serpent will strike the heel of the woman's descendant, but he will strike the serpent's head, which one of them will be the victor?

Note: This judgment on the serpent has long been seen by Jews and Christians as the first hint of a promised Savior for mankind.

14. What does God mercifully prevent by banishing Adam and Eve from the garden where they might eat from the tree of life (verses 22-24)? (Imagine what the world would be like if Adam and Eve and all their descendants were to live unendingly in their present condition.)

*Note: Death causes a separation between us and whatever dies. The death of a person ends any further communication with that person. The Bible says **God is spirit** so God does not have a physical body, but we human beings have both a spiritual and a physical dimension.*

Physical death is only a part of the separation that God predicted would be the consequence of disobedience. Disobedience makes us spiritually dead toward God, cut off from fellowship with him. Adam and Eve began all human beings' separation from God.

Summary

1. Describe the major differences between the situation in Genesis 2:8-25 and that in 3:7-24.

2. What happens that destroys the peace of the garden?

3. From this Genesis account, whose fault was it that human beings sinned?

Why do you think that?

God made human beings *in his own image* with the capacity and freedom to make choices, but with choices came responsibility and the consequences of those choices. For example, we have the freedom to choose to drink poison, but not to decide the result of drinking it. We can choose not to recognize or obey God, but we cannot escape the results that follow from that choice.

Cutting ourselves off from God, the source of life, results in death and all the miseries that accompany it. The world is in its present condition because human beings, who chose to rebel against God, are experiencing the results of their choices.

From the way God treated Adam and Eve, we see that he is both just and merciful. In a time for silent prayer you may want to ask God to help you recognize how you have rebelled against him and made choices that have separated you from God.

In preparation for the next study:

To understand how the disobedience of Adam and Eve spread, read Romans 1:18-32. Work through the questions in Discussion 5.

DISCUSSION 5

How Did the Trouble Spread?

Adam and Eve were driven from the garden for their disobedience, and their descendants have continued to disobey God. In his letter to the Romans, the Apostle Paul's description of the first century world reveals the results of each generation's rebellion. Much of it sounds like current news headlines.

Read Romans 1:29-32. As you read, look for similarities to our present-day civilization.

1. In this list of sins, can you find any that people do not commit today?

2. Why would such behavior arouse wrath in a morally perfect God?

Read Romans 1:18-28, looking for reasons for God's anger.

3. This passage explains why the world has come to this awful state and the reasons for God's wrath toward humankind. What specific things about the Creator can all human beings discover by observing his creation (verses 19, 20)?

Why can't we plead ignorance or innocence before God?

Note: God's wrath is never irritable or self-indulgent, as human anger often is. It is the steadfast and absolute opposition of a just judge and righteous ruler toward evil.

4. What response does God desire and expect of each of us because of what he has made plain (verse 21)?

   Even though confronted with this evidence about God, how have people reacted?

   How does this reaction compare with that of Adam and Eve in Genesis 3?

5. Verses 21, 22 say that people's *thinking became futile* and their *hearts were darkened* and *foolish*. As a result, in what foolish ways do people act (verses 23, 25, 28)?

   What illustrations do you see today of the behaviors named in verses 23-25?

6. What examples of not thinking it *worthwhile to retain the knowledge of God* (verse 28) do you see in modern life?

7. Three times the phrase is repeated, *God gave them over to*…(verses 24, 26, 28). In each case, what reasons are given for why God let people go downhill, doing whatever they wanted?

   What had human beings done to bring about such action by God (verses 23, 25, 28)?

8. To what does God *give them over* (verses 24, 26-28)?

   How has living by those desires affected our culture today?

9. How would our responsibility be different if it said that *God caused them to...* rather than that *God gave them over to...*?

   How do our thinking, emotions and actions all contribute to our guilt before this righteous, holy God (verses 18, 21-23, 28)?

10. How are the things listed in verses 29-32 natural consequences of *futile* thinking, a *foolish heart* (verse 21) and a *depraved mind* (verse 28)?

11. Do you think God's decree in verse 32 is reasonable?

    Why, or why not?

Summary

Some people blame God for the state of the world: "If God exists, why doesn't he stop wars, crime, famine, etc.?" What does Romans 1:18-32 teach about the root cause of such situations?

Adam and Eve choose not to believe what God said and rebel against him. The result is spiritual and physical death. Such rejection of God and his commands has led to all other kinds of evil. Our world is in its present condition because men and women, rebelling against God, experience the results of their choices. ***Although they knew God, they neither glorified him as God nor gave*** *thanks to him, but their thinking became futile and their foolish hearts were darkened* (Romans 1:21).

Even though Adam and Eve choose their own way, resulting in death, God loves them and reaches out to help them. Take time now for silent prayer. You may want to tell God if you recognize in yourself some of the attitudes and actions listed in Romans 1:29-32. If you are sorry for not honoring God as God, for not believing him or not obeying him, you can ask for forgiveness, knowing that God is listening, and understands all your thoughts and motives.

In preparation for the next study:

To discover what God does about this problem of evil, study carefully the Bible sections listed in Discussion 6. Use the questions provided to help you.

DISCUSSION 6

What Did God Do About The Problem?

We have seen that God the Creator made human beings to have fellowship with him and to care for his creation. Their choice to disobey God caused estrangement from God, and brought spiritual and physical death to the whole human race. However, God promised a solution, saying it would come through a descendant of the woman.

Although human beings were responsible for their separation from him, God planned a way to communicate with them, to rescue them and restore them to fellowship with him. In this study, look for the beginning of God's solution to the problem, and how God chose to communicate with human beings.

What is the purpose of *words*? Keep in mind your answer to this question as you read what the Gospel of John says about *the Word*.

Read John 1:1-4, 10, 11, 14-18

1. What facts do you learn about *the Word* from verses 1-4?

2. What else do you learn about *the Word* from verses 10, 11, 14-18?

3. Jesus Christ made God the Father known to us (verses 17b, 18). What connection do you see between the fact that Jesus does this and his being called *the Word*?

Note: History records that Jesus was born about two thousand years ago, lived some thirty-three years and was put to death on a Roman cross. The writer of the Gospel of John, one of Jesus' twelve disciples who traveled with him for three years, observed his actions and learned from him. As an eyewitness of Jesus' ministry, John concluded that Jesus Christ was the Creator God who became a man to reveal himself to us. In this study we shall consider what Jesus said about himself and what he did to substantiate those claims.

*The **John** mentioned in verses 6, 15 was Jesus' cousin, the son of Elizabeth and Zechariah (Luke 1). Six months older than Jesus, John (known as John the Baptist) preached a baptism that expressed repentance and pointed toward Jesus' coming after him (Mark 1:2-8).*

Read John 8:48-59

Note: Abraham, the father of the Jewish people, lived about two thousand years before Jesus was speaking.

4. What does Jesus claim for himself that no mere man could ever say (verses 51, 54, 55)?

What amazing claim does Jesus make in verse 58?

*Note: In the Old Testament one of the names by which God identifies himself is **I am**. Jesus uses that name for* *himself in this sentence. The Jews are shocked and outraged at what they see as blasphemy. According to Jewish law, blasphemy was to be punished with death by stoning.*

Read John 10:24, 25, 30-39

5. What do the Jews again understand Jesus to be claiming?

Note: In verse 34 as part of his argument with the Jews, Jesus quotes Psalm 82:6, in which God called "gods" human rulers and judges who were to act as his representatives.

6. According to Jesus, what do his miracles reveal about him (verses 24, 25, 37, 38)?

7. How does Jesus want his listeners to respond to his miracles?

Read John 14:6-11 to see other claims by Jesus.

8. In this section Jesus talks with his disciples who want to understand him, rather than with his opponents. What claims does Jesus make about himself in verse 6?

9. What does Jesus say about the relationship between God and himself?

How do Jesus' claims in this section contradict those who say that Jesus never claimed to be God?

Note: Neither the prophet Mohammed, nor Buddha, the teacher and philosopher, ever claimed to be God.

10. What response does Jesus desire?

Read Mark 1:30-34, 40-42; 4:35-41, looking for actions that back up Jesus' claims.

11. It is easy to talk, but Jesus acts to validate his claims. Over what kinds of things does Jesus demonstrate his power in these verses?

12. What similarity is there between the method God used to create the universe (Genesis 1:3, 6, 9, etc.) and what Jesus does to calm the storm (Mark 4:39)?

13. Why would the disciples suddenly fear Jesus so much (verse 41)?

Read John 11:17-48, 53

14. What confidence in Jesus do Mary and Martha have from previous experience (verses 21, 32)?

15. What claim does Jesus make in verse 25?

    How does he substantiate that claim in this incident?

16. By what method does Jesus raise Lazarus from the dead?

17. What does Jesus want to reveal to the people by calling Lazarus back to life (verses 40-43)?

18. What do the Jewish leaders admit about Jesus (verse 47)?

How do they respond to this evidence (verses 48, 53)?

Summary

1. What have you learned in this study about:

    who Jesus claimed to be

    what Jesus did to back up his claims

2. Today we may be like the Jewish leaders of Jesus' day, determined not to believe regardless of the evidence. Or, we may be like Jesus' disciples who kept listening and looking for an answer to the question, "Who is this?" What helps you keep an open mind as you examine the evidence about Jesus?

Spend some time in silent prayer. Perhaps you would like to ask this person who is **the way and the truth and the life** to lead you further in knowing him.

In preparation for the next study:

To consider the evidence for Jesus' resurrection, read carefully the Gospel of Matthew 27:57—28:15, and the Gospel of John, chapter 20. Study through the questions for Discussion 7 before the next meeting.

DISCUSSION 7

Did Jesus Really Come Back from the Dead?

Jesus claimed not only to have been sent by God, but to *be* God himself, and he backed these claims with his life and miracles. A number of times, Jesus told his disciples he would be rejected by the religious authorities and killed, but that three days later he would rise from the dead. In today's study sections, look for what happens to fulfill Jesus' predictions. What evidence do these accounts offer that Jesus actually rose from the dead?

Read Matthew 27:57-66 for details of Jesus' burial.

1. What is done with Jesus' body after his death?

   What precautions are taken to secure the tomb, and why?

Note: The seal represented the authority of the Roman empire. Breaking the seal could bring the death penalty.

Read Matthew 28:1-15

As you read, find what each group of people says or thinks has happened to Jesus' body. Imagine the feelings of at least one of the groups.

2. What do Mary Magdalene and the other Mary see at Jesus' tomb?

3. What specific statements does the angel make about Jesus?

   How are these statements confirmed for the two Marys?

4. The angel, the women, the guards, and the Jewish leaders all recognize that Jesus' body is *not* in the tomb. How do their explanations of this fact differ?

5. Could you have believed the story the guards tell? (How much can you see when you are sleeping?)

*Note: The Gospel of Luke (24:9-12) says that the Eleven disciples and others with them do not believe the reports of the women that Jesus has risen from death, **because their words seemed to them like nonsense**. Obviously the disciples are not eagerly expecting the resurrection, nor are they grasping at any excuse to believe it.*

Read John 20:1-10

6. What thoughts do you think Peter and John (***the other disciple***) have as they run toward the tomb?

   What possible explanations could there be for the burial cloths (verses 6, 7) being there without the body?

7. John saw this and *believed* (verse 8). What do you think he believed?

Note: Verse 9 is an explanation of why they had not believed earlier.

Read John 20:19, 20, 24-31, noticing how and when Jesus appears to the disciples.

8. What evidence for his resurrection does Jesus give the disciples by his actions in verses 19, 20?

    What evidence does Jesus give by his specific offer to Thomas who has set his personal conditions for believing (verses 24-29)?

Note: After Jesus died on the cross, a soldier pierced his side with a spear (John 19:33, 34).

9. What does Thomas come to believe (verses 27, 28)?

10. According to verses 29-31, what is John's purpose in writing this account?

    What will *you* have by believing that Jesus is the Christ, the Son of God?

Summary

God, the all-powerful, holy, wise, loving Creator, sent his Son, *the Word*, to communicate with rebellious, unbelieving humankind. Jesus' claims and actions, including his resurrection, are evidence to help answer the basic question, "Who is Jesus?" His resurrection is the clearest proof of Jesus' deity, as well as evidence of the fact that he met our basic need for deliverance from death, the result of human sin. The Bible says this resurrected Jesus is the living God, that he is the one who created us, has put his hand on us and wants to lead us.

1. Thomas had honest questions as he heard the evidence about the resurrection from the other disciples. Jesus understood Thomas' doubts and lovingly confronted him. Thomas responded with, **"My Lord and my God!"** What questions do you want to ask as you consider the evidence about Jesus?

2. John wrote his account so that **you may believe that Jesus is the Christ, the Son of God, and that by believing you may have life in his name** (20:31). Take a short time for prayer, telling Jesus your honest response to him at this time.

In preparation for the next study:

Read carefully the Bible sections listed in Discussion 8. Use the questions provided to help you understand why Jesus had to die.

DISCUSSION 8

Why Did Jesus Have to Die?

It is not surprising that the one who is the source of life and who created everything should also be able to overcome death as he predicted. But *why* did Jesus have to die? Why would he permit his own execution? In this study to help you answer these questions for yourself, we look at the circumstances surrounding Jesus' death.

Read Mark 10:32-34, 45

1. As Jesus approaches Jerusalem, he describes to his disciples what will happen to him there. List the details that Jesus predicts about his arrest, trial and death.

2. What does Jesus say is the purpose of his life and his death (verse 45)?

Note: In Jesus' day, **ransom** *meant the buying back of people from slavery, captivity or death by paying a price.*

3. From what you have studied in the first six discussions, why do people need to be ransomed?

How are people in slavery, captivity, or death in today's culture?

What are your thoughts as you consider that Jesus knew that he was to give his life as a ransom for you?

Read Mark 14:43—15:39, looking for details of how Jesus dies.

4. In what ways are Jesus' detailed predictions in 10:32-34 carried out?

5. On what charge is Jesus condemned (14:60-64)?

   Why?

6. By whom is Jesus deserted, betrayed or rejected?

   14:43-45, 50, 64, 65, 66-72

   15:15, 16-20, 29-32, 34

7. What impresses you about how Jesus behaves toward the religious and political leaders?

   About how he faces his death?

Note: **Elijah** *(15:36), the greatest of the Old Testament prophets. According to Jewish legend, he would return to save Jews in great danger.*

The curtain of the temple *(15:38), the heavy woven curtain that separated off the holiest part of the temple into which only the High Priest entered once a year on the Day of the*

Atonement. **Torn in two from top to bottom** *(15:38) at the moment of Jesus' death (Matthew 27:53)—the way into God's presence was now open to all.*

Read Isaiah 52:13—53:12
Isaiah, an Old Testament prophet about seven hundred years before Jesus, foretold the coming of the Christ (Messiah).

8. According to 52:13—53:3, what will God's Servant (the Messiah) be like, and how will he be treated?

9. In verses 4-6, what reasons are given for the Messiah's suffering?

   For whose transgressions and iniquities is he afflicted?

10. What do the Messiah's punishment and wounds provide for us?

11. Whose idea is it to do this (verses 6, 10)?

Read 1 Peter 1:18-21; 2:21-25
The Apostle Peter, one of Jesus' twelve disciples, writes to the early Christians referring to Isaiah 53.

12. What does Peter say about why Jesus died?

13. In what ways is Jesus who died on the *tree* (cross) like the Messiah predicted in Isaiah?

14. According to Peter, what does Jesus' death for us accomplish (1:18; 2:24, 25)?

Summary

The coming of Jesus to be the Messiah (Christ), the Savior of the world, was predicted by prophets in the Old Testament. Two thousand years ago God became a man and entered our history in order to die in our place, for our sin. Spend a few moments in prayer, telling God your response to what he has done for you. In closing, have someone read aloud Philippians 2:5-11.

In preparation for the next study:

Discussion 9 is the conclusion of the series. Prepare carefully, using the questions provided to think through what you have discovered in the first eight studies.

DISCUSSION 9

The Point of It All

What is the Significance of Jesus' Crucifixion?

The first eight studies in this series have traced the central theme of the Bible. With the aid of a diagram, this last lesson examines how the Bible explains the meaning and importance of the death of Jesus Christ.

Defining The Problem

As you quickly look back over what you have discovered up to this point, you lay the foundation for understanding what Jesus' death can mean for us now.

1. What did you learn about the God of the Bible in Discussions 1 and 2?

    What kind of God is he? Describe him.

    What has God done (Genesis 1; Psalm 139)?

2. God made man in his image as the climax of his creation. In what ways are the man and woman he created *like* God?

    How are they *not* like God?

What was their relationship with God when he first created them?

3. What contact or relationship, if any, does God have with people now (Psalm 139:1, 5, 10, 17, 18)?

4. In Discussions 3 through 5 we learned that something terrible happened to break our relationship with God. How did the first man and woman both use their wills *not* to glorify God as God (Genesis 2:15-17; 3:1-6; Romans 1:21)?

    What happened as a result (Genesis 3:7-24; Romans 1:21-32)?

5. Put in your own words what it means to be *dead* toward God.

    For further help in understanding this, read Isaiah 59:1, 2; Romans 3:10-18.

Note: The problem, then, is that the people whom God created to know him and have delightful fellowship with him are estranged from him. Sin has made an impenetrable barrier.

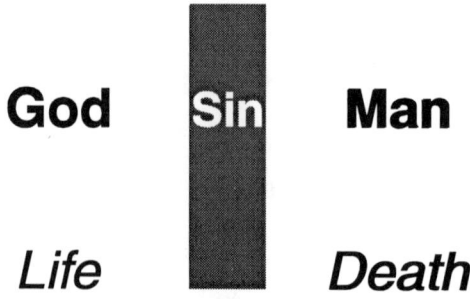

The Point of it All

What Did God do to Solve the Problem?

Three characteristics of God help us better understand why God himself became a man and died in our place.

Read Isaiah 6:1-5

God's holiness is so perfect and intense that even angels hide their faces. Because God is totally without sin or darkness, he is completely above and apart from sinful human beings.

6. If holiness were God's only attribute, what would be the reaction of a perfectly holy God toward a person who is sinful?

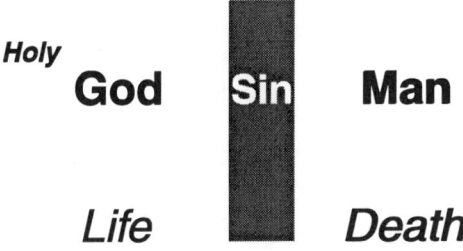

Deuteronomy 32:4—*...his works are perfect, and all his ways are just. A faithful God who does no wrong, upright and just is he.*

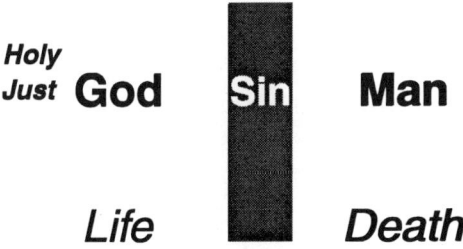

7. Since God is perfectly upright and just, what would his justice require him to do when someone has rebelliously disobeyed the law, his command?

1 John 4:8— *God is love.*

8. How do you think a perfectly loving God would respond toward one of his creatures who has sinned?

What would God's love prompt him to do?

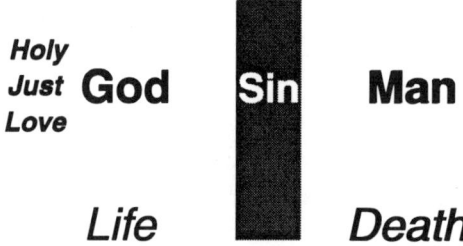

These three attributes of God—holiness, justice and love—at first glance seem to demand irreconcilable things. To act in harmony with his own character, God's holiness cannot ignore the sin or welcome the sinner. His justice must punish the law-breaker. Yet his love would want to forgive and reconcile. The last three discussions revealed what God did to solve this seeming dilemma.

The Solution

Discussions 6 through 8 showed how very much God cares for us and what he has done to reveal that caring.

Thinking of God's love, notice in the following verses how much God sacrificed for us.

Philippians 2:5-8—*Christ Jesus,...being in very nature God, did not consider equality with God something to be grasped, but made himself nothing, taking the very nature of a servant, being made in human likeness. And being found in appearance as a man, he humbled himself and became obedient to death—even death on a cross!*

1 Peter 2:24, 25—*He* Christ *himself bore our sins in his body on the tree, so that we might die to sins and live for righteousness; by his wounds you have been healed.*

2 Corinthians 5:21—*God made him who had no sin to be a sin offering for us, so that in him we might become the righteousness of God.* (Alternate reading, NIV)

9. What did Jesus give up, and to what extent did he humble himself?

10. What was Jesus *bearing* on the cross?

    For whom was he a substitute?

11. What did Jesus accomplish by humbling himself to death on the cross?

Romans 6:23—*The wages of sin is death, but the gift of God is eternal life in Christ Jesus our Lord.*

12. What wages does sin earn?

    In contrast, how does one get eternal life, and from whom?

    Through whom does this eternal life come?

1 John 2:2—*He is the atoning sacrifice for our sins, and not only for ours but also for the sins of the whole world.*

(Alternate reading, NIV) —*He is the one who turns aside God's wrath, taking away our sins, and not only ours but also the sins of the whole world.*

13. In God's sight, how effective is the death of Jesus?

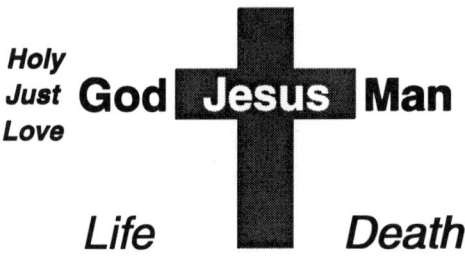

Our sins have been put on Jesus on the cross. Jesus' death dealt with the root of human-kind's estrangement from God. In Jesus Christ, a loving God has given himself in place of human beings who deserve to die. A just God has acted justly by punishing sin with death. A holy God is now free to have fellowship with those whose sins are gone.

Our Response

Read aloud Romans 6:23 together, thinking about the gift of God.

God solved the problem that separated us from him and opened up the way back to himself. However, God made us with a free will, and he will not force anyone to accept the gift he offers. He waits for our response.

Read John 1:11,12; 3:16-18, 36; 5:24, noticing the words which express the response for which God is waiting.

14. What is *God's* part in our salvation?

    What is *ours*?

15. If I do not respond personally to what God has done, what is the result for me?

As the diagram shows, by what he did at the cross Jesus has become the "way" to God, a bridge from Death over to Life. If we receive Jesus as Savior and Lord, our sins are forgiven, we are reconciled to God and become his children, and we have eternal life.

If you want to receive Jesus Christ, or later when you are alone, here is a simple prayer you could use. Any equivalent words will do.

> *Lord Jesus Christ,*
> *I am a sinner, asking to be forgiven.*
> *Believing you died for me, I accept your forgiveness.*
> *I receive you as my Savior and Lord.*
> *Thank you for dying for me.*
> *Thank you for making me your child.*

Take a short time for silent or spoken prayer to give anyone who would like to respond to the Lord Jesus Christ an opportunity to do so.

Review and Summary

Read the following verses, noticing what this says about those who have believed.

Romans 10:9,10—*If you confess with your mouth, "Jesus is Lord," and believe in your heart that God raised him from the dead, you will be saved. For it is with your heart that you believe and are justified, and it is with your mouth that you confess and are saved.*

If *you* believe in your heart that God raised Jesus from the dead and you are willing to say that he is *your* Lord, perhaps you can take the next step by telling someone about it.

If you wish to continue your study of the Bible, we recommend the Gospel of Mark as your next study. To order copies of the Neighborhood Bible Studies guide on Mark, contact NBS by phone: 1-800-369-0307 or email: nbstudies@aol.com. For more information and samples, visit our web site: www.neighborhoodbiblestudy.org.

What Should Our Group Study Next?

New Groups and Outreach Groups
How to Start a Neighborhood Bible Study
Mark *(recommended as first unit of study)*
Foundations for Faith
Acts, Book 1 and Book 2
John, Book 1 and Book 2
Four Men of God *(Abraham, Joseph, Moses, David)*
Lenten Studies
Luke
Romans
1 John and James
Genesis, Book 1 and Book 2

Groups Reaching People from Non-Christian Cultures
Foundations for Faith
Genesis, Book 1 and Book 2
Mark or The Book of Mark *(Simple English)*
Four Men of God *(Abraham, Joseph, Moses, David)*
Romans
1 Corinthians
Lifestyles of Faith, Book 1 and Book 2
Luke

Advanced Groups/ Sunday School (Adult and Older Teens)
Matthew, Book 1 and Book 2
Courage to Cope
Four Men of God *(Abraham, Joseph, Moses, David)*
1 & 2 Peter *(Letters to People in Trouble)*
1 & 2 Thessalonians, 2 & 3 John, Jude
Haggai, Zechariah, Malachi *(Prophets of Hope)*
Ephesians
Colossians
Philippians
Prayer
Relationships
Treasures
2 Corinthians
Galatians & Philemon
Isaiah
Servants of the Lord
Work - God's Gift
Lifestyles of Faith, Book 1 and Book 2

Biweekly or Monthly Groups
They Met Jesus *(8 Studies of N.T. Characters)*
Celebrate
Courage to Cope
Psalms & Proverbs
Coping With Stress
Set Free
Servants of the Lord
Work - God's Gift
Lifestyles of Faith, Book 1 and Book 2
Relationships
Treasures

1-800-369-0307 • www.NeighborhoodBibleStudy.org

About Neighborhood Bible Studies

Neighborhood Bible Studies, Inc. (NBS) is a leader in the field of small group discussion Bible studies. Since its founding in 1960 by Marilyn Kunz and Catherine Schell, NBS has pioneered the development of Bible study groups that encourage each member to participate in the leadership of the discussion.

The **ministry** of Neighborhood Bible Studies provides people with the opportunity to discover the truths of Scripture for themselves. Through these small group discussion Bible studies, men and women:

> encounter Jesus Christ
> choose to obey him
> mature in faith.

NBS **methods** and **materials** are used around the world to:

> equip individuals for facilitating discovery Bible studies
> serve as a resource to the church.

Skilled NBS personnel conduct workshops and seminars to train individuals, clergy and laity in how to establish small group Bible studies in neighborhoods, churches, workplaces and specialized facilities. Publication in more than 25 languages indicates the use of NBS cross-culturally.

Churches from a wide range of denominations use the NBS materials and methods to:

> develop a program of outreach Bible studies
> give electives for high school and adult classes
> build support groups within the church fellowship to encourage spiritual nourishment.

About the Authors of Foundations for Faith

Virginia Bowen and Lorraine Fleischman spent over 35 years in Japan as missionaries. Together with a number of Japanese Christians they founded Seisho o Yomu Kai (SYK), the Japanese expression of Neighborhood Bible Studies, and directed its work until their retirement in 1987. SYK continues under Japanese direction. The Japanese edition of *Foundations for Faith* is available from the Dobbs Ferry office.

COMPLETE LISTING of NBS STUDY GUIDES

Getting Started
How to Start a Neighborhood Bible Study *(handbook & video)*

Bible Book Studies
Genesis, Book One *Beginnings with God*
Genesis, Book Two *The Shaping of a People*
Psalms & Proverbs *Perspective and Wisdom for Today*
Isaiah *God's Help Is on the Way*
Haggai, Zechariah, and Malachi *Prophets of Hope*
Matthew, Book One *God's Promise Fulfilled*
Matthew, Book Two *God's Purpose Fulfilled*
Mark *Discovering Jesus*
Luke *Good News and Great Joy*
John, Book One *Believe and See*
John, Book Two *Believe and Live*
Acts, Book One *A New Beginning*
Acts, Book Two *Paul Sets the Pattern*
Romans *A Reasoned Faith...A Reasonable Faith*
1 Corinthians *Finding Answers to Life's Questions*
2 Corinthians *The Power of Weakness*
Galatians & Philemon *Fully Accepted by God*
Ephesians *Living in God's Family*
Philippians *A Message of Encouragement*
Colossians *Staying Focused on Truth*
1 & 2 Thessalonians, 2 & 3 John, Jude *The Coming of the Lord*
1 & 2 Peter *Letters to People in Trouble*
1 John & James *Faith that Knows and Shows*

Topical Studies
Celebrate *Reasons for Hurrahs*
Coping with Stress *Insights from Eight Bible Leaders*
Courage to Cope *Uncommon Resources*
Foundations for Faith *The Basics for Knowing God*
Lenten Studies *Life Defeats Death*
Prayer *Communicating with God*
Relationships *Connected to Others: God's Plan*
Servants of the Lord *Living by God's Agenda*
Set Free *Leaving Negative Emotions Behind*
Treasures *Discovering God's Riches*
Work - God's Gift *Life-Changing Choices*

Character Studies
Four Men of God *Unlikely Leaders*
Lifestyles of Faith, Book One *Choosing to Trust God*
Lifestyles of Faith, Book Two *Choosing to Obey God*
They Met Jesus *Life-Changing Encounters*

Simplified English
The Book of Mark *The Story of Jesus*

Other Resources

Share the Joy! Group News

This quarterly newsletter for small group members contains inspiring stories as well as information designed to help you have a more rewarding group experience. Includes topics such as principles of adult learning, group dynamics, inductive Bible study, and discovery learning. It also provides current information on NBS ministries and materials.

To view the current issue and to order copies for your group, visit our web site: **www.neighborhoodbiblestudy.org** or contact us directly.

Neighborhood Bible Studies, Inc.
56 Main Street
Dobbs Ferry, NY 10522
1-800-369-0307
nbstudies@aol.com

For Churches:
The Small Group Bulletin

A quarterly bulletin insert written to motivate church members and attenders to become involved in a small group, and to promote small groups as a biblical means to grow in faith through discipleship, evangelism, Bible study, ministry, support, missions, education, and worship. It contains short stories, handy tips, and reviews of other small group resources.

To see the current issue and to place orders, visit our web site: **www.neighborhoodbiblestudy.org** or contact us directly. (Our address information is provided above.)

The Caramel Popcorn Venture

By Jamie A. Brown & Meg Seitz
Illustrated By Arody J. Victoria

Bea is for Business: The Caramel Popcorn Venture

Text: Copyright © 2014, Bea is for Business, LLC
Illustrations: Copyright © 2014, Bea is for Business, LLC

All Rights Reserved.

Bea is for Business and all story elements, illustrations, characters, and logos are trademarks of Bea is for Business, LLC.

No part of this book may be used or reproduced in any manner whatsoever without written permission from the publisher, except in the case of brief quotations embodied in critical articles and reviews.

Published by:

Bea is for Business, LLC, P.O. Box 33336, Charlotte, NC 28230

For more information and educational resources,
please visit: www.beaisforbusiness.com

ISBN 978-0-9893403-4-2 (pbk) - ISBN 978-0-9893403-5-9 (ebook)

First Edition 2014

To my grandmothers, who—in ways big and small—paved the way. J.B.

With love to my Gram, Grace Steele Doczy, University of Pittsburgh MBA, Class of 1943—revolutionary and inspirational for generations to come . . . xo. M.S.

Wow, my first chapter book—to my assistants Ariana and Giancarlo, and always my inspiration, Neyda, my wife! A.V.

Authors' Note:

Creating and writing this first chapter book for Bea is for Business has been a blast! What's made it even more of a fun adventure is connecting with our young readers—some of whom read early drafts of this book on their own and others who worked with generous parents who helped collect thoughts, feelings and feedback for us to make this book even more impactful.

We are especially grateful to this team for their valuable insights. These chapter books are for you. And they wouldn't be the same without you.

Thank you to Sydney, Mia, Ariana, Kaela, Isabella and Nolan.

#BEAwesome

What is a Hashtag?

A hashtag is a word or phrase starting with the # symbol that puts thoughts or messages into categories for easier online searching.

Examples:

#Happy—means you're talking about something happy!

#Victory—means you're talking about something you won, or were victorious in!

People use hashtags for Twitter, Facebook and other types of communication online. A lot of times, Bea uses hashtags in the book to help get across how she is feeling. #LearnSomethingNew (Hey—that means you just learned what a hashtag is!) #GreatWork

Contents

Chapter 1 - The Business of Bea is for Business   9

Chapter 2 - Drooling   19

Chapter 3 - CEO   27

Chapter 4 - Market Research   37

Chapter 5 - A or B   47

Chapter 6 - Hitting the Right Spot   57

Chapter 7 - Caramel's Up!   65

Chapter 8 - Show Stopper   75

Chapter 9 - Teamwork   85

Chapter 10 - Calling in Sick   93

Chapter 11 - Divvy Up   101

Chapter 12 - High-Five   109

Chapter 13 - Your Project!   117

Chapter 1

The Business of Bea is for Business

You know that feeling when you run so fast that your feet pulse in your sneakers and your heart feels like it's going to burst out of your chest? That's how I feel right now.

Every day when the teacher opens the door for recess, our class races to the giant—and I mean GI-ANT—boulder at the far right-hand corner of the Henry Phipps Elementary School playground. We call that boulder King Coal.

Today, I was the first one to make it to King Coal. (And I ran with my messenger bag, too!) #Victory

My new friend, Matty St. Clair, bolted out right behind me. He and I are meeting up at King Coal. He helped me with my science fair project, so now we're teaming up to get him started on a pretty cool business idea he had.

The two of us sit cross-legged on the rough edge of the gigantic rock. I yank my Big Ideas notebook out of my messenger bag. The notebook knocks a charm on my bracelet.

The charm jingles. It is a miniature slice of chocolate cake with strawberry-pink icing. Mom bought it for me so I'll always remember the party-planning business I helped start with my friend, Makayla.

Thinking about that business makes me think about MY business: Bea is for Business.

I stand on my tiptoes on top of King Coal to

see if, by some wild chance, I can see my Bea is for Business office in my backyard. I slip a bit, but I catch myself. It's just a wee bit too far.

"What are you doing, Bea?" Matty asks.

"I was just trying to see if I could see my new office," I say.

"Wait," Matty asks. "You have an office?"

"Sure do! Two weeks ago, my dad and I converted his toolshed into a new office for me. Dad calls it an 'upgrade' from my old office upstairs in our house."

"That's pretty cool," Matty says.

I explain to Matty how my dad and I gave the toolshed a complete makeover. First, we cleaned out the cobwebs and donated all the old tools. Then, we painted it with a fresh coat of Klondike-white paint. Dad installed electronic hook-ups out there, too, so I can use my tablet any time. Having the extra space has been awesome for Bea is for Business.

As I sit back down, I flip to page 23 of my Big Ideas notebook. Page 23 is the next blank page. I've got to explain to Matty this idea I've started for him. He asked me for a fun, new marketing idea for his lawn care business.

"Matty, I'm thinking lawn care business handouts," I say. "Handouts that can be hung on every doorknob in the neighborhood."

I draw out what the handout could look like and what it should say. I turn my Big Ideas notebook to the side and hold it out for us both to see. #LookingGood

"I love the idea, Bea," Matty says. "I'll start on that tonight after my homework!"

Matty gives me a high-five and runs to the four square game across the playground.

'I love the idea.' That's exactly what I like to hear. My business's mission is to help other kids with their businesses.

Here's how it works. First, a friend comes to

me with a business idea or a business problem. We talk it through and come up with ideas to get it moving. Often, we end up starting a new business. It's a BLAST! I mean, just THINK about what's possible?!

As I close my Big Ideas notebook to run over to the blacktop, it occurs to me that I told Mrs. Murdstone, the librarian, that I had a book about construction equipment at home. I keep forgetting to return it. I hope it's under my bed. I draw a star on my hand with my pen to help me remember. I don't want to pay the late fee. I'm saving my money.

At the end of the day, the bus drops me off on the corner of Commerce and Washington. I throw my earbuds into my messenger bag and run home. In fact, I run all the way home—through the front door and up to my bedroom, first door on the right. I slip off my sneakers. I lie down like a star on my fuzzy, red rug. My dog, Hamilton, runs into my room.

"Hey Hamilton," I say. "I missed you today!"

Hamilton sweeps his tongue all over my face. He loves me that much. I love him, too. He's my dog-brother.

Mom comes to the door and leans on the doorframe. She laughs watching me and Hamilton play-wrestle. I stop and sit up, brushing back the hair that's fallen out of my pigtails.

"I bought you something today, Bea," Mom

says, handing me a small paper bag.

I gently pull out a card. There's a quote on the front of it.

The quote reads:

Think of yourself as on the threshold of unparalleled success. A whole, clear, glorious life lies before you. Achieve! Achieve!

At the bottom is the name: Andrew Carnegie. (That means he is the guy who said the quote.)

"That's your guy, Mom!" I say.

My mom is a tad obsessed with Andrew Carnegie stuff. He's got a really cool business story. He was born into a very poor family and he became very, very, very rich over his lifetime, through a lot of hard work in several businesses.

"Yes, it's an Andrew Carnegie quote," Mom smiles. "It basically means you can do anything you set your mind to, Bea. Cool, isn't it?"

"It is pretty cool," I say, tracing the letters with my finger. "Thanks, Mom. I've got the perfect place for it."

I crawl on my hands and knees over to my messenger bag, toss open the flap and slide the card inside. Hamilton sniffs my bag. He probably smells the handful of gummy squirrels I keep in a plastic baggie in the front pocket.

As I pick up my messenger bag, I see the star on my hand.

"Oh! The library book!" I shout. I double-back and dive under my bed. The book, *86 Fun Facts about Construction Equipment,* is right there.

Whew! I think to myself. *I'll return that to Mrs. Murdstone tomorrow.*

I race Hamilton all the way down the stairs, through the kitchen, and out to my Bea is for Business office.

My office has two small windows in the front and bright orange marigolds in the planter boxes beneath each window. I keep a key to the office tucked in the planter box on the left. I find the key and unlock the door.

Inside, there's a big bulletin board my dad and I built together.

I gently pull the Andrew Carnegie quote out of my messenger bag. I pin it to my bulletin board. I step back to read it one more time. I hear bird feet patter across the tin roof. That gets me thinking.

I tap the toe of my shoe. Now, I'm in brainstorming mode.

What if I collect rainwater off the roof to water the marigolds in the flower boxes?

What if I start a business that takes rainwater from the roof to people who need it?

What if I pop the toolshed roof open to look at the stars with the telescope I got last year?

What if I design a pulley system that runs from my bedroom window to my office?

This one really gets me thinking. *What if. . . .*

Chapter 2

Drooling

It's 11:36 a.m. the next day. It's lunchtime. I'm running late because I needed to return that library book. My friends waited for me, so now we have to find our way to a small, round table in the back of the lunch room. The light above the table flickers on and off. This might be the worst lunch table ever.

My friend, Gracie Goldman, pulls a chair over from an empty table to scoot in next to me.

"What's for lunch today?" I ask Gracie,

pointing to her lunchbox. Gracie brings her lunch in an old, tin lunchbox that's covered with superheroes.

"It's my favorite—a turkey and pimento cheese sandwich with a side of banana," she says. "Oh wait! Grapes today!" She shakes a bag of plump green grapes.

"I've got one of my favorites, too—cream cheese and strawberry jelly," I smile.

I squirm around in my chair, leaning to the left, so I can reach into my back right pocket. That's where I keep my change. I pull out 60 cents. Perfect. Just enough for dessert.

"What kind of cookies are they selling today?" I ask Gracie.

"I think I saw oatmeal raisin on the sign up front," Gracie says, chewing her sandwich.

"Yuck," I say as I slouch down in my chair. I like oatmeal raisin cookies about as much as I like chocolate covered ants.

Just then, I see Gracie pull the most delicious looking chocolate chip cookies from her lunchbox. Two chocolate chip cookies! I start to drool.

"I'm probably only going to eat one of these," Gracie says.

"What? Really?" I ask. "Well, can I pay you for it? I've got 60 cents." I extend my hand to Gracie.

"Don't be silly. We're friends," Gracie says. "Save your 60 cents for when we want to split a Pirate Paulie's Cinnamon Pretzel!" We both laugh. We LOVE Pirate Paulie's Cinnamon Pretzels!

Gracie hands me a cookie. I bite into it. It's even better than I could have imagined.

"Ho-ly YUM!" I shout, cookie crumbs popping out of my mouth. I cover my lips and look around because I'm afraid I said that too loud. The fifth graders at the next table start to giggle at me.

"Where did you buy this, Gracie?" I ask, studying what's left of the cookie.

"Actually I made them with Grandma Pippa," Gracie says. Gracie's Grandma Pippa lives with Gracie, her mom and Gracie's sister.

"I don't think I've ever had a cookie this good," I say, shaking my head in disbelief.

"I love cooking and baking," Gracie says dreamily. "I like to think of it as my superpower." Gracie taps her finger on her superhero lunchbox.

"Minor problem, though," she continues, snapping back to reality. "Our mixer broke when we made these cookies last night. Mom says it's not worth repairing and we can't afford a new mixer right now."

"That's terrible," I say. "You've just GOT to make more of these!"

"I know," Gracie says. "But, to buy the new

Baby Blue Benedum Mixer I want, I would need $200."

I pause. I know all about the Baby Blue Benedum Mixer. I've seen it pinned to my mom's online bulletin board.

"Those are awesome mixers," I confirm. At the same time, we both sing:

"Nothing mixes it up like a Baby Blue Benedum Mixer!"

We both laugh. We've heard the commercial

dozens of times. The fifth graders turn around and giggle at us again.

"Mom was helping me look for a cheaper one to buy online, but they're just not the same, you know?" Gracie says, shrugging. "Then again, two HUNDRED dollars—that's SUPER expensive."

"It sure is," I say. I don't even know if I've ever seen $200 in person.

"My mom made a deal with me—she said that if I could pay for half of the Baby Blue Benedum Mixer, that she would pay for the other half," Gracie says. "But, earning even $100 seems impossible."

I watch as Gracie stuffs her plastic containers and baggies back in her lunchbox. She seems upset.

"Are you okay?" I ask.

"Yeah, I'm fine. I just would love to figure out a way to get that mixer," she says.

"Why don't you figure out a way to earn the

money?" I ask.

Gracie doesn't answer.

"Listen, I know you don't have a mixer for baking, but you love to make things in the kitchen, right?" I say.

"Yes," Gracie replies, listening closely.

"So, what if you made something else that doesn't need a mixer. Something you could sell. Then you could earn the money to buy your Baby Blue Benedum Mixer while doing something you love," I say.

Gracie nibbles another corner of her cookie. She scrunches up her nose. She's thinking.

"You know, that's not a bad idea," she says. Gracie is fiddling with something on her lunchbox.

"What is that?" I ask.

She holds it in her palm. It's a keychain with a chef's hat.

"Grandma Pippa got it for me last summer on

a food tour in California," Gracie answers.

It was all I needed to see: Passion. Gracie's passion made me feel like I wanted to be a part of her business. I mean, don't we all want to be part of something that someone is excited about? I knew I wanted to help her.

#GameOn!

Chapter 3

CEO

I race home from the bus stop. Just as I'm about to grab the doorknob, the door opens. It's Mom.

"Whoa! Oh hey, Mom!" I say, trying to scoot around her to get to my office.

"Slow it down, Bea. We've got an errand to run," she says, closing the door behind her.

"But I just got here and I've got A LOT of work to do and A LOT to tell you!" I say. I'm a tad annoyed.

"I've got to get this envelope in a CEO's hand in Austin, Texas, by 10 a.m. tomorrow," Mom says. She's holding a big, black and gold envelope.

"What's a CEO?" I ask.

"Chief Executive Officer," Mom replies. "The person who runs a company."

"He's a big deal, then?" I ask.

"She. And yes," Mom answers.

I'm kind of bummed I can't start working right now, but it's Mom and it's her business. And our family is a team.

We hop in the car, and I fasten my seatbelt. "Mom, I don't get it," I say. "Texas is like six states away, and . . . " I look at my watch, "it's 3:32 p.m. How will that envelope make it to Texas by 10 a.m. tomorrow?"

"You can pay more money to have mail shipped or flown somewhere for next day delivery," Mom says.

Mom pulls the car into a parking spot in front of Shipperz. We walk right up to the counter.

"Hi, I'd like to ship this envelope out for delivery tomorrow to Austin, Texas by 10 a.m.," Mom says to the cashier.

"Sure thing," the cashier says. "That will be $25.42."

The cashier busily punches buttons. Mom hands him a card from her wallet.

"Debit is fine," Mom says. Every time she says 'debit,' she always types in her PIN code. It's a secret number.

Mom looks relieved when she hands the envelope over to the cashier. It'll make it on time.

"Question, Bea," Mom says, as we head back to the car. "If you could have any veggie side for dinner tonight, what would it be?"

"Brussels sprouts, Ma," I reply, re-fastening my seatbelt. "I know what I want to talk about at dinner tonight, too," I say.

"Really, what's that?" Mom asks.

"I want to launch another business," I say.

Mom looks in the rearview mirror and smiles. "Brussels sprouts and business. Sounds good to me!"

That evening, I help Mom and Dad set out dinner.

As Dad settles in at his seat, he looks up from his plate. "I hear you've got another business up your sleeve, Bea," he says.

"I do!" I confirm. "Gracie Goldman wants to earn money to buy a Baby Blue Benedum Mixer."

"Those are quite the mixers!" Dad says, looking at Mom. "So, what's the plan to earn the money?"

"Well," I say, taking a deep breath. "That's our first problem. We need to make something to sell that doesn't need a mixer."

"Sounds like making something simple would be smart," Mom jumps in. "Plus, you'll want to make sure it's not too expensive to make."

I nod my head as I take another serving of Brussels sprouts. Mom's right. We have to think about costs. We've got some serious business planning to do. I eat quietly, listening to Mom's advice.

At the end of dinner, Mom looks over at me. "Bea, if you want to help Gracie earn the money, you can do it. I know you girls can. You both can be CEOs, you know."

That night, I have the sweetest dreams ever. Literally, sweet dreams of baking with Gracie.

I dreamt that Gracie and I were making gigantic vats of sweet treats. We poured gooey dough onto a conveyor belt. It was an assembly line that made gobs of different types of treats

at once! Gracie and I tasted everything right off the line.

Then, my alarm goes off. I stumble out of bed and into the bathroom. I spit out my toothpaste and look in the mirror.

I realize that to end up with enough money for the mixer, we'd actually need to earn more than $200. Since I'll be splitting the work with her, and we'll have expenses, we're going to have to aim high.

This will be the most I've ever tried to earn with a business. That scares me. I'm also scared because we don't know what kind of business we should start.

The only thing I do know: If Mom thinks we can do it, I think we can, too.

At school, I slowly take off my windbreaker and hang it up in my coat cubby. I see Gracie doing the same.

"Morning, Gracie," I smile. "Are you ready to

be CEO of your own business?"

"CEO?" Gracie asks, her eyes wide.

"Yep. Chief Executive Officer. We're going into business so you can earn the money to buy that Baby Blue Benedum Mixer," I say.

"Really?!" Gracie looks so surprised.

"I want to help you earn it," I confirm.

As we walk down the hallway to art, I tell Gracie about my dinnertime brainstorming session with Mom and Dad.

"Gracie, what's something you already love to make that's easy and not that expensive to make?" I ask.

Gracie thinks a minute. Then she rattles off a few ideas. "Cookies, brownies, snack mix, muffins . . . and on rainy days," she says, "Grandma Pippa and I make caramel popcorn."

"Wait, wait, wait!" I shout, holding my hand up high. "Caramel popcorn?" I ask. I L-O-V-E caramel popcorn.

"Yeah," Gracie says. "It's pretty simple to make. It's delicious and our family gobbles it up every time."

Those are two good things to hear: simple and delicious. #Jackpot!

"What if I help you build a business where you sell caramel popcorn to earn money to buy the Baby Blue Benedum Mixer?" I ask.

Gracie scrunches up her nose. She's thinking. "I . . . I love it," she says. She seems surprised by her own answer.

"My mom and I have to go to the grocery store after school today," I say. "We could pick you up and do some popcorn research."

"I'm in," Gracie says.

She's starting to sound a lot more like a CEO.

Chapter 4

Market Research

After school, Mom picks Gracie and me up from the bus stop. We drive to the Market Square grocery store and walk inside. I look up and see gigantic signs with pictures of food that label each of the aisles.

One reads: SNACKS. Jackpot.

We make our way down the aisle toward the popcorn kernels. I take a step back to look at everything. There's a lot to take in. I start tapping the toe of my shoe. I'm thinking. I'm

thinking about how completely overwhelming this is. #WhereToBegin

"Hey, I've got an idea," Mom says, sensing that I don't know where to start. "Bea, you've got your Big Ideas notebook, right?"

"Yeah . . . it's right here," I say, pulling my notebook out of my messenger bag.

"Write down the names of the popcorn kernels and the prices. Don't forget to write down their sizes in ounces, too," she says. She points to where we can find the ounces on each bag. "You'll need to make sure you pick a bag of kernels that's a good price for how much you're getting."

We look the kernels over closely. Some are a lot more expensive than others. Some are really inexpensive—but they look browner and kind of yuck-o, if you know what I mean. No one wants to eat yuck-o popcorn.

We want good quality kernels, but we also

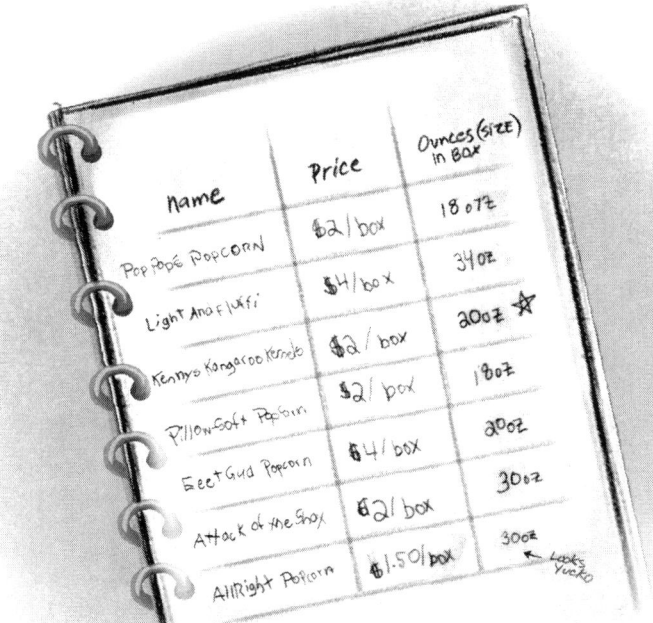

don't want to spend too much money on the kernels, or our caramel popcorn will be too expensive to make.

Gracie and I walk down the aisle. We write down seven different brands of popcorn kernels with their names, prices and sizes in ounces.

"How about these?" I turn to Mom.

Mom takes the bag and scans it over. "In one sentence, tell me why you like these," she says.

"The kernels look like a good size and they're cheaper than some of these others," I say, pointing to the expensive bags.

"I think that is a good decision," Mom says.

We've chosen a brand of kernels called Kenny's Kangaroo Kernels. They're $2 a box.

Printed on the box, it reads "Kenny's Kangaroo Kernels. We'll hop and pop right into that bowl." I get it. That's clever.

Mom says we'll probably need five boxes of Kenny's Kangaroo Kernels.

That's $2 x 5 boxes = $10.

Then, we figure we will need to buy caramel popcorn ingredients and little bags. We estimate that will be another $10.

Mom agrees to loan us $20 to buy our supplies. I write the loan amount in my Big Ideas notebook. Gracie and I will have to pay my mom back $20 after we sell the popcorn.

It kind of stinks that we're already borrowing money to start the company. But, I know deep down it's the cost of doing business.

I toss the last box of kernels into the cart. Just as the box lands, I see Nigel DeFault. He and his mom are coming down the aisle. They're coming right toward us.

Nigel has his head down playing with a shiny, silver smartphone. He was showing it to everyone at school today, calling it "The Thunderbolt."

Nigel and I have been in the same class since Kindergarten. He's a bit uptight and snobby sometimes, and a bully all the time. He wears suit coats and button-down shirts. And he LOVES technology. Whatever's new and shiny and popular—Nigel gets it.

It's a good thing I see him before he sees me. This gives me a couple seconds to prepare myself.

"Hi, Mrs. DeFault," I say. His mom hired me and my friend, Makayla, to plan Nigel's younger brother's fourth birthday party, so she's really supportive of Bea is for Business.

"Well, hi Bea, hi Gracie. What are you two doing?" Mrs. DeFault asks.

"We're here with my mom," I say. "Gracie and I are working on selling caramel popcorn to help her buy a Baby Blue Benedum Mixer." I motion toward Gracie.

"That's a pretty nice mixer," Mrs. DeFault adds. "Nigel's dad loves the one I bought him for his birthday."

"Wait! Caramel popcorn?" Nigel chimes in. "You've got to be kidding me."

Mom returns and starts to talk with Mrs.

DeFault. That leaves Gracie and me eyeball-to-eyeball with Nigel.

"I don't get why you do stuff like this, Bea," Nigel barks. "I mean, people can come to a store like this or shop online—then they can buy caramel popcorn at the same time they buy all their other groceries."

"Look, Nigel," Gracie responds. "Our popcorn will be fresh AND homemade."

"That's fine, Gracie, but where are you going to sell it?" Nigel asks. He raises both of his arms in the air.

I start to sweat.

"We've got some ideas, but we're not ready to share them right now," I say.

"Whatever. Good luck with all that," he says, shaking his head. He glues his eyes back on his smartphone and wanders down the aisle.

I know Nigel really bothers Gracie. They worked on a project together at school last year. Gracie ended up doing a lot of the work. That's why Gracie barked right back at him.

As we walk to the register with my mom, I look over at Gracie. Her eyes are filling up with tears. Our run-in with Nigel exposed some questions about the business that we don't have answers to yet.

"Hey, Gracie, when we start this business, what are we going to call it?" I ask, hoping to get her mind off Nigel.

Gracie wipes her face. "I was thinking about naming it after my Grandma Pippa."

"Grandma Pippa's Popcorn," I say. "I like the sound of it."

"Or what about Pippa's Popcorn," she says, smiling.

"Pops by Pippa?" I add.

"Pippa Pop?" Gracie says, laughing. There aren't any tears in her eyes now. She's back to thinking about business.

Chapter 5

A or B

Mr. Rich's math lesson today is clicking for me. He's writing problems on the Smartie Board, and I'm writing the answers down in my notebook faster than he can even get to the next one. This whole multiplication thing is making a lot of sense.

Suddenly, I feel something tap my shoulder blade. It feels like a pencil eraser.

As Mr. Rich turns to the board to write another problem, I look over my shoulder. My classmate hands me a piece of crumpled up paper—with my name on it. I open it up quickly so I don't make any crinkle sounds.

Bea,
News flash: I've got TWO caramel popcorn recipes. Meet at my house after school? Turn around and shoot me a thumbs up if you're in.
-Gracie

I quickly glance over my shoulder to give Gracie a thumbs up. She nods back at me.

The second the school bus pulls over at my stop, I hop off, tighten the laces on my 412 sneakers, and run home.

"Mom!" I yell, sliding down the hallway and into the kitchen. "Gracie asked if I could come over today and make caramel popcorn with her and Grandma Pippa. Can I? Can I?"

"Sure sweetie," Mom says.

"We're going to make two different recipes of caramel popcorn and taste them to see which one is better!" I say excitedly.

"That's a great idea, Bea," Mom says. "Why don't you make up a little survey and have some of your friends try it, too? Then you can get their feedback, and sell whichever recipe is better."

Okay. A survey is a list of questions that ask opinions about something. I remember my mom got one after visiting a doctor's office. I know what a survey is. #Jackpot. But making one myself? #Bamboozled

"How do we make a survey?" I ask.

"Good question," Mom says. "You could make a simple A and B survey. Grab your tablet, and we'll quickly write one up together."

Mom says she'll type if I talk.

"All right, tell me some things you'd like to know about your popcorn recipes," Mom says.

"I want to know which one tastes better," I state.

"Good, so let's make sure we ask about the overall taste," Mom says. "Why don't you ask about the sweetness and the saltiness of the recipes too?"

"Jackpot!" I say. "AND what about even the crunchiness of the popcorn?"

"Yes, that's perfect!" Mom confirms as she

types.

I know if people can answer these questions for us, we'll be able to figure out which recipe is better to use so we can sell more popcorn.

The survey ends up looking like this:

Which popcorn has a better buttery taste? **A or B**
Which popcorn has a better caramel flavor? **A or B**
Which popcorn has a better crunchy texture? **A or B**
Which popcorn has a better salty flavor? **A or B**
Which popcorn has a better sweet flavor? **A or B**
Which popcorn do you like better overall? **A or B**

I print out enough surveys for some friends to fill out. Then, Mom and I walk down the street to Gracie's house. Gracie and her grandmother meet us at the door.

"Hi honey!" Grandma Pippa shouts, as she scoops me up for a hug. Grandma Pippa is the coolest grandmother ever. She goes to hot yoga twice a week, and she flies to Italy every June. I think Gracie is so lucky to have her grandmother around all the time.

"Hi Grandma Pippa, hi Gracie," I say.

We walk into the kitchen. Gracie and Grandma Pippa have set out all the ingredients and the two recipes.

"I brought these, too," I say, holding out the recipe surveys.

"What are those?" Gracie asks.

"They're surveys so we can get feedback on which recipe people like better. We can text Matty St. Clair, Lander, and Makayla to come fill them out. Then, we can look at their feedback and know which caramel popcorn is better to sell!" I say.

Gracie is digging the idea. In fact, she shoots off the texts to our pals faster than I can even get settled.

I take a good look around the kitchen. Grandma Pippa watches me.

"You know, honey," Grandma Pippa says,

putting her arm around me, "I raised my two kids—Gracie's mom and her Uncle James—here."

"Wow," I say. Grandma Pippa sure has lived here a long time. "Launch any businesses from this kitchen yet?" I ask, climbing onto a stool at the counter.

Grandma Pippa laughs. "Lots of good ideas around the kitchen table. But, this will be the first business launch. What do you say we get started?!"

Once we finish making the two batches of caramel popcorn, we set the bowls out on the counter. Gracie and I turn our backs while Grandma Pippa swaps around the bowls. Now ONLY Grandma Pippa knows which recipe is in which bowl. #Secret

Finally, Grandma Pippa puts a little card by each bowl. One says "Bowl A" and the other "Bowl B."

Just then, the doorbell rings. Matty St. Clair, Lander, and Makayla are all standing at Gracie's front door. Within five minutes, Gracie's mom and older sister arrive home from ballet. We suddenly have a bunch of taste testers!

I watch quietly as our taste testers munch the popcorn and fill out their surveys.

"Which one do you think will win?" Lander asks.

"I love this one!" Matty St. Clair says as he points to the popcorn marked "Bowl B."

"This one here, though, was so crunchy!" Makayla says. She gobbles another handful.

Everyone samples the recipes and completes the surveys. I collect all the surveys into one pile. I know I need to give a point for every time A is chosen on the survey to Bowl A. Every time B is circled, I should give a point to Bowl B. Whichever bowl has more points is the winner!

I tally up the points:

Bowl A: 12

Bowl B: 30

Bowl B was the clear winner!

(That was my favorite one, too!)

I see Grandma Pippa wink at Gracie. We know Bowl B won, but we don't know which recipe Bowl B had in it. Only Grandma Pippa knows.

"Which one was it?!" Gracie and I jump up and shout.

"Looks like you picked a good recipe," she says. "You know, that's our long-time family recipe."

"Bea, it was Grandma Pippa's recipe!" Gracie says. "It's perfect. I've wanted to call the business: Pippa Pop."

"Jackpot! Let's make her the face of the brand! We can make copies of a photo of Grandma Pippa and glue the pictures to each popcorn bag we sell!" I suggest. #GetCreative

I love everything about where this business is going. We have a taste-tested, friend-approved product. We have a fantastic popcorn name: Pippa Pop. We have a neat bag design idea including Grandma Pippa's photo.

Now we've just got to sell it!

Chapter 6

Hitting the Right Spot

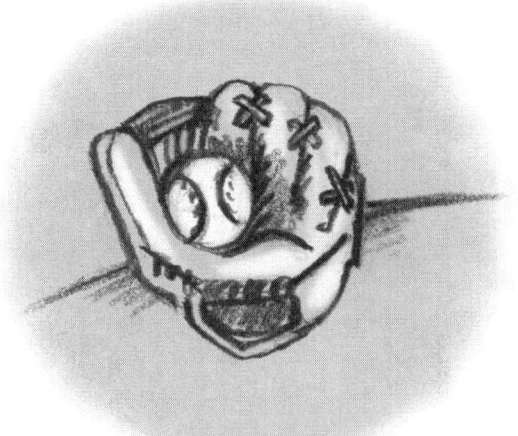

When Gracie comes over to my house the next day, we head out to my office. As we're walking through the backyard, I can hear Gracie talking, but I'm not really paying attention. I'm deep in thought.

"Earth to Bea!" Gracie says.

"Oh, hey, I'm sorry. I was thinking," I say, snapping back to reality.

"Yeah, I see that. I was talking to you, and you weren't listening," Gracie says. #Honesty

Gracie's right. I wasn't listening to her. I wasn't even paying attention. That's not good for business.

"What's on your mind?" she asks, closing the office door behind her.

I point out the toolshed window toward my bedroom window.

"See that window up there? That's my room. I've been thinking about how to design a pulley system with a bucket to be able to pass things from my bedroom to the toolshed."

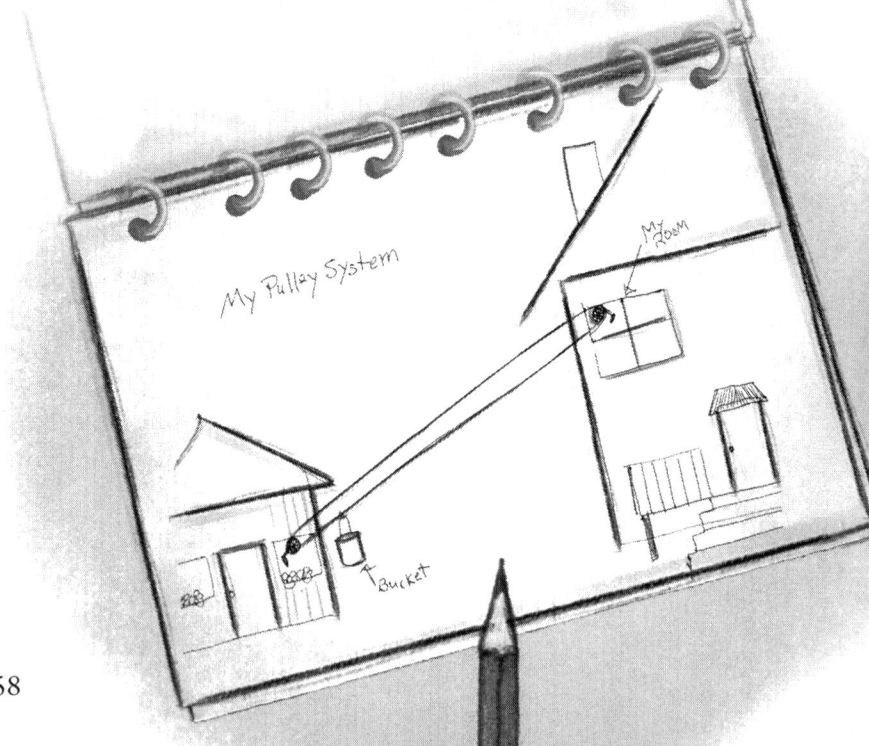

"Why can't you just walk stuff down to your office?" she asks.

"I could. That's what I do now. But, I think there's a better way. See, look at this drawing." I show Gracie my Big Ideas notebook with my drawing of the pulley system I saw in the *86 Fun Facts About Construction Equipment*.

She looks it over for a minute. Then, she looks up at me. "Bea, that's really awesome."

"Thanks! I have a whole list of ideas. This just seems to be the one I can't figure out. I think that's why I'm so fascinated by it, you know?" I say.

Gracie's face is completely bamboozled. I guess it IS pretty awesome.

We settle into our chairs around the table.

"Let's chat about how we're going to sell Pippa Pop Caramel Popcorn," I say, flipping to a fresh page in my Big Ideas notebook.

"So, I've been thinking," Gracie says leaning

back in her chair. "We've got to figure out where people like to eat popcorn."

"You're right. We've got to hit the right spot. Let's start with this question," I say. "Where do people most like to eat popcorn?"

We brainstorm together. I write all the ideas down.

We've got a bunch of them:
the movies
festivals
fairs
on a boardwalk
amusement park
at home on the couch
baseball games
basketball games
outdoor mall
the park

I yank the list from my Big Ideas notebook, tearing it along the spiral side. I slide out of my chair and pin the list on my bulletin board.

"Here, let's step back and look at the whole

list," I say.

Gracie and I back away from the table and look at all the places we've written down. Our eyeballs are racing all over the paper. I pop a handful of gummy squirrels in my mouth. I chew. And I think.

"I've got it!" I shout. "Lander told me his older cousin is playing in the town's baseball tournament next weekend at the Point Park Fields. A bunch of teams from all over the region are coming in for it. There will be a ton of people!"

"That's perfect!" Gracie says. "We should be able to sell a lot of popcorn there. I know a couple of the fields are right in the middle of everything."

"Great. That sounds like it might be a good place to set up," I say, thinking it all through. "We should also make a sign so people know what we're selling."

Gracie agrees.

I get out all my art supplies—and I have a lot of art supplies. There's puffy paint, stickers and markers in every color. I have construction paper, glitter glue and a stencil set.

We get started on a large piece of white poster board. We stencil out the business name: Pippa Pop.

Gracie is about to finish coloring the second P in Pop, when she stands up at the table.

"Hey! I wonder if the baseball fields would

let us make an announcement about our business at the tournament!" Gracie says.

"What do you mean? On the loud speaker?" I ask.

"Yeah, on the announcer's microphone," Gracie confirms.

I take a big, deep breath. If there's one thing on Earth that I hate to do, it's to speak in front of people.

"Ah, if you're willing to do that," I say, "I think that'd be a great idea."

"I'll look into that," Gracie says. "I know Mr. Morgan, and he announces a lot of the baseball games."

I look up to see that Gracie is making a list. I got her started with a Big Ideas notebook like mine. Now she keeps all her ideas in one place.

I look down at our sign. It's looking pretty top-notch. It's fun and bright and colorful. For a single business meeting, we've made a lot of progress.

We know where we're going to sell: the Point Park Fields during the tournament.

Plus, we have a couple of ideas to help us with marketing our business: a business stand, a sign, and hopefully, an announcement over the loud speaker. That's the one I'm leaving entirely up to Gracie.

As I stand next to the table, I flip through the pages of my Big Ideas notebook. I find the drawing of my pulley system again. I won't have time to work on it now. There are more urgent matters—like Gracie's business.

Very carefully, I tear out my pulley system drawing. I pin it up on my bulletin board. My eye skims across the wall. I read the Andrew Carnegie quote that Mom gave me.

I tap it with my left pointer finger. "Achieve, achieve . . . ," I whisper.

Chapter 7

Caramel's Up!

I wake up that next sunny Saturday morning to a giant kiss from Hamilton. I blink my eyes shut again.

"Wait!" I sit straight up in bed. "Hamilton, we've got a business to launch today!" I smile.

Gracie and I decided that if we're going to sell fresh popcorn, we have to make it as fresh as we can. So, we're going to make all the caramel popcorn with Grandma Pippa this morning. That way the caramel popcorn will be fresh for us to sell this afternoon, and also Sunday afternoon. Well, that's assuming we don't sell out on the first day. #ThinkPositively

Our official goal? To earn a total of $220.

Gracie and I decided to set a high goal and split the money. If we set a goal to earn $220, we could pay my mom back the $20 she loaned us, and then each get $100. With Gracie getting half of $200, that'll be enough for her to pay for her part of that Baby Blue Benedum Mixer.

Mom pokes her head in my bedroom. "All decked out in your money-making green, I see," she says.

"I am." I loop my belt through. "Do you think we can actually make $220, Mom?"

"I'm not sure," Mom says. "That's a lot of money. But one thing is for sure, you won't make any money just sitting here." She winks at me. "And don't forget, have some fun!"

When I arrive at the Goldman's house, Grandma Pippa and Gracie are drinking green smoothies, listening to oldies music, and setting up the kitchen for our big production day. We're off to a good start, and it's a good thing. We've got a lot of caramel popcorn to make, and we've got a lot of bags to fill up, too.

Right away, I watch Grandma Pippa put the corn kernels in a big yellow pot. She closes the lid. She stirs the hot, gooey caramel mix that's bubbling on another stove burner.

We're making Grandma Pippa's family recipe again—the one that won the taste test!

Gracie and I hustle to prepare the packaging. First, we put a sticker label on each bag. We printed them off the computer. They read:

PIPPA POP
Caramel Popcorn
Sweet. Fresh. Homemade.

We leave room for a photo. Gracie found a photo of Grandma Pippa, so we made some black and white copies of it on the copier at the school library. (High-five to Mrs. Murdstone for the help!) I already had cut the pictures out, and mounted them to colorful pieces of paper. Now we're gluing them to the paper popcorn bags.

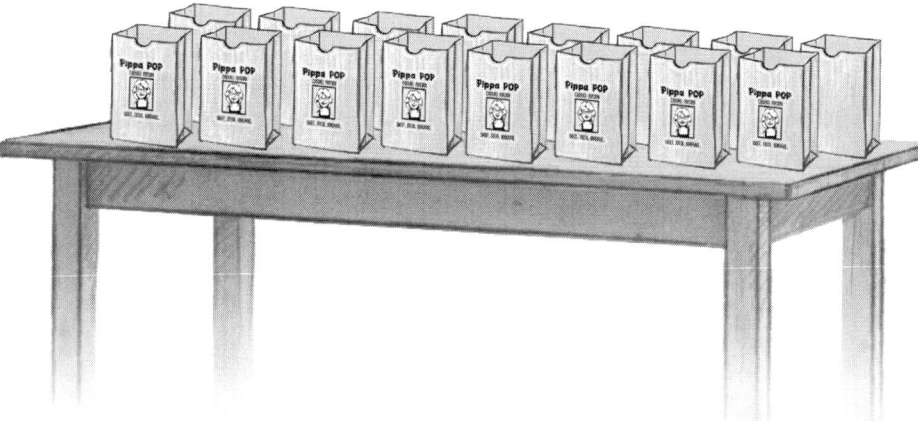

Grandma Pippa turns on the stovetop, and the pot starts to heat up. We gather close, listening for the first "pop!" sound.

The pops start slowly. Just one at a time. The tiny kernels are bursting into fresh airy bits of popcorn. Across the room, Gracie and I hurry to finish decorating our final bags, sipping the last drops of our green smoothies.

"Caramel's up!" Grandma Pippa says.

"Bea, the caramel is ready!" Gracie says excitedly. "This is my favorite part."

Gracie and I hop back up on the counter and watch as Grandma Pippa pours the buttery caramel mix over the top of the popcorn. I'm wondering how many times Grandma Pippa has made this recipe.

Once all the caramel is mixed over the top of the popcorn, Grandma Pippa rinses her hands and pats them dry on her jeans.

"Let me see what you girls have done over here," she says, walking over to all the bags we've decorated.

"Grandma, yes, come see!" Gracie says, hopping down from the counter. "Do you see your picture? It's on every one of the bags!"

"You girls amaze me," Grandma Pippa says. "You really do. When I was a little girl, people told girls they could only be certain things—like nurses or teachers or secretaries."

I wait for her to continue her list.

"What else?" I ask.

"Honey, that was about it," Grandma Pippa says.

We stare at her. Neither of us says anything. The world sure has changed a lot.

"You're lucky, you two, you've got so much ahead of you," she says, "and I admire the confidence you two have to just get out there and make things happen. Think of all the things you could do . . . ."

I see Grandma Pippa run her hands over our paper popcorn bags. She's thinking about something.

"All right, girls," Grandma Pippa says, jumping up quickly. "Let's get you ready for selling popcorn this afternoon!"

Gracie looks over at me. "How much do you think we should charge for each bag of popcorn?" she asks.

"I think we should charge $5," I say. I point at a calculation in my Big Ideas notebook. Then I poke numbers into my calculator.

1 box of kernels makes 10 bags of popcorn
SO
5 boxes of kernels make 50 bags of popcorn
50 bags x $5 = $250

"If we sell ALL 50 bags of popcorn at $5 each," I continue, "we'll make $250. That's more than our goal! It will be plenty of money to split so you can get your mixer!"

Gracie looks over the calculation.

"Sounds great to me," Gracie says. "I just cannot believe how quickly you can figure all that out, Bea."

Just then we hear Grandma Pippa stirring up

the popcorn. It's ready.

"Looks like it's about time to pack it all up," I say. "Let's do an assembly line to put them all together, one by one."

Gracie holds a bag open while Grandma Pippa spoons popcorn into the bag. When the bag is about two-thirds full, Gracie passes the bag to me.

My job is to fold over the top of the bag and tape it shut with a little piece of colored tape. Then I place all the finished bags in a pile to my side. We work through them, one after the next.

We're finishing up when I hear a car horn toot outside Gracie's house. It's my dad. He's taking us to the baseball fields to sell our popcorn this afternoon.

"Do we have everything, Gracie?" I ask. I run down the list with my finger. "The big box of caramel popcorn bags?"

"Check," Gracie confirms.

"Sign?"

"Check," Gracie says.

"Small table?"

"We've got it," Gracie says.

"Then I think we're good to go," I confirm.

Grandma Pippa pokes her head around the corner. "Hugs?" she asks.

Gracie and I run into her arms.

#NowWeAreReady

Chapter 8

Show Stopper

I've never seen these baseball fields SO packed. Dad has to drive around the parking lot twice before he can find a spot.

"Where do you girls want to set up to sell your popcorn?" Dad asks.

"The busiest spot possible," I say. "Maybe right over there between those two ball fields."

I point far out to the left. There are two

games happening at the same time. It looks like it could be a really busy spot.

Gracie and I creak open our folding table. I attach our sign to a fence behind us with string. Then, we set up our popcorn inventory. We arrange the bags in neatly organized rows and store the extras under the table.

"Bea, I see Mr. Morgan," Gracie says, looking over toward the announcer's box.

Sure enough, there he is, climbing up the wooden stairs to take his place for the game. Mr. Morgan is one of the fifth grade teachers. He always announces the home team's baseball games.

"Are you going to go ask him?" I ask Gracie.

"Absolutely!" she says, running across the field towards Mr. Morgan.

I continue to straighten up our inventory as I watch Gracie out of the corner of my eye.

She and Mr. Morgan shake hands. Their heads nod. He hands her the microphone.

"Ladies and gentlemen," she says. "Fresh, homemade caramel popcorn is for sale between the two fields! Pippa Pop Caramel Popcorn is $5 a bag. Play ball, and eat caramel popcorn!"

I'm stunned. How did she do that? She just walked up there and belted out a perfect sales pitch. She even mentioned the brand's name!

Someday, I think to myself. *Someday.*
#RoomToGrow

A new game begins, but we're not selling popcorn quite as fast as I'd like. We have our sign, and we made our loud speaker announcement. We also have a great product. But still, where are all the customers? Why isn't everyone buying our popcorn?

Everyone just seems hunkered in their bleacher seats, and they're not moving.
#Problem

Deep down, I'm counting on the seventh inning. That's when the parents all get up, walk around, and grab snacks. We should sell a lot of inventory then. Otherwise, we're going to end up taking a whole lot of popcorn home.

Soon enough, the innings pass, the score is tied four to four, and we find ourselves in the middle of the sixth inning.

"Gracie, it's almost time for the seventh inning stretch!" I say.

I look around. We've got a lot of popcorn to sell to hit our goal. I stand up and straighten out all the inventory. We're preparing for a seventh inning rush. But we aren't prepared, at all, for what is about to happen.

All of a sudden, three middle schoolers show up and plop down their own business—selling ice cold soda and water! And they're just 35 feet from us!

"WHAT. IS. THAT?" I say to Gracie out of the corner of my mouth.

Gracie does a double take.

This is our territory, I think to myself. *We are about to get to the seventh inning stretch with a real shot at selling a bunch of inventory, and these jokers come and set up their business? It's not fair!*

This seriously could be a business show stopper.

"What are we going to do?" Gracie whispers.

I look over our inventory. We've got a long way to go to sell all the bags. Okay, we do still have tomorrow. But we've got so many more bags to sell today to reach the goal.

"I don't know what to do," I say. "Do you have any ideas?"

Gracie thinks a minute. I do, too.

"We could get more aggressive and shout out that we have popcorn," Gracie suggests.

"We could also take our sign down and walk around the stands," I say.

"Or we could find another location," Gracie says.

I'm thinking hard.

"Here's what we're going to do," I say. "We're going to stay the course. We're going to stay here, and we'll get aggressive when the crowds come out during the seventh inning stretch."

We look closer at our new competition. They're selling a lot of different drinks—water bottles, sodas and juice. I'm not going to lie—it's a smart idea. It looks really refreshing for this warm day—probably more enticing than caramel popcorn.

Plus, the kids selling are much older than us. The girl is wearing cool sneakers. And the boys' hair is all swoopy with gel in it. You know what

that means—sixth graders.

Just then, a chime signals the seventh inning stretch. There's a lot of chatter coming from the stands. People are shaking hands and making their ways down through the bleachers. The crowd begins to trickle out toward us.

Some people are buying popcorn. But, all I can see are the people who choose the drink stand instead of us!

I think about how many MORE people

would be buying popcorn if it wasn't for those kids over there selling drinks. They're stealing our customers!

That's when bad grows worse.

I hear the faint ring of a scooter's bell. I know that bell all too well. That scooter's bell belongs to Nigel DeFault.

Not now, I think to myself.

"Hey girls," Nigel says. He rings the bell on his scooter three times fast. We call that scooter Black Friday. It's so sleek and smooth. I'd never tell Nigel this, but it is the fastest scooter in the neighborhood.

"Hi Nigel," I say.

"What are you two doing?" he asks.

"Selling caramel popcorn," I reply. I'm secretly hoping that the shorter my reply, the shorter he'll hang around.

"Oh! Was this the cute, little idea you two were working on the other day at the grocery store?" he asks.

"Yes," I say. "I'm sorry, excuse me, Nigel. I need to help this customer."

I hand the customer a bag of popcorn. He hands me a $5 bill. We both say, "Thank you."

"That's really nice, Bea," Nigel says. "It looks like you've got a lot left to sell, huh? Nothing's popping today?" Nigel snickers.

"We're doing fine," I confirm.

"Well, I'm kind of thirsty," Nigel says. He pauses and looks at our table. "Are you selling any drinks?" he asks.

"No, Nigel," I reply. "Just caramel popcorn."

"That's too bad, Bea. I'm going to head over there to that stand. They've got drinks and that's exactly what I need on a hot day," Nigel says, scooting away.

I drop my head to the table. I peer out of one eye. I see all the popcorn we still need to sell.

Chapter 9

Teamwork

News flash: the seventh inning doesn't give us the sales spike we needed. At all. We're officially in trouble.

I can't help but think about the opportunities we're losing because of that drink stand that plopped down. #Frustrating

Dad stops over. He's drinking water from a water bottle.

"Dad! Where on Earth did you buy that

water? You didn't buy it from those kids did you?" I bark.

"Uh, no, I brought this from the car, Bea. Slow it down. What's wrong?" he asks.

"It's not good," I say. "We're not doing well at all." I can barely speak. I pull Dad aside.

"Dad, those kids just set up over there, and they're taking our customers," I say.

He looks over at the other business stand. I want him to rush over and knock it down. I want him to yell at them and tell them it isn't fair. He doesn't.

"Sweetheart, don't worry about them," he says. "Believe in yourself and your business."

"But, we're losing customers because of them," I say.

"There's a way to make a win-win situation," Dad says. "Just think it through. Think about how you can both succeed."

Just then, a friend of Dad's walks up and pulls

him into a conversation. I'm tapping the toe of my shoe. I'm thinking. I get an idea—a really BOLD idea.

I walk over to the drink stand.

"Hi, I'm Bea Banks," I say, stretching my hand out to one of the boys. He sets down a water bottle and reaches his hand out to shake mine.

"Hi, I'm Henry Ford," he says.

"Henry Ford? Like the guy who invented the assembly line?" I ask.

"You're smart. Yeah. No relation though," Henry responds. I look Henry over. He doesn't seem as scary as he looked from our business stand. Up close, he doesn't look that much older. There's not that much gel in his hair.

"Henry, I was wondering if you wanted to put your stand next to ours and sell together," I say.

"Um, yeah," he says. "We can set up right next to each other. We can try that."

I don't know what to say. I'm just in shock he

said yes. I guess you never know what an answer will be until you ask.

"You definitely chose the smartest spot, Bea," Henry says. "We'll move our stand closer to you. Let me get my friends to help."

"Okay," I say. "Come on over."

Henry and his friends move right next to us, and the five of us start to work—together. In fact, one of Henry's friends goes into the bleachers and shouts, "Popcorn, drinks for sale!"

Suddenly, we have a line—and instead of people choosing popcorn or a drink, they are starting to buy both! We all start making more money!

Gracie and I have to shuffle back and forth between getting caramel popcorn bags and taking money from customers. We're moving fast. We're working together.

I lean over to Henry.

"I really like your idea to sell juice and water

bottles," I say. "I might try that sometime."

"They're easy to sell on a warm day," Henry says. "But, your popcorn is homemade. That's awesome."

Gracie jumps in. "Bea, we've almost sold through half of our popcorn inventory!" she says. "That means we're getting close to reaching half of our goal!"

Gracie looks really happy. Visions of that Baby Blue Benedum Mixer are dancing in her head.

"Are you trying to save up to buy something?" Henry asks.

"I'm trying to earn $100 so I can pay for my half of a kitchen mixer I want," Gracie says.

"Neat," Henry says. "I want to save up for a scooter. There's this awesome black scooter that I absolutely love. My mom says I have to earn all the money for it."

Just then, Nigel stops over.

"Looks like you still have a lot of inventory left over, Bea," Nigel says.

"We do," I say. "But we're about to reach our goal for the day. We'll have the rest of the inventory to sell through tomorrow."

"Probably just luck," Nigel grumbles as he scoots away.

I look over at Henry. His mouth is wide open. He's staring at Nigel.

"That was the scooter. That was the exact scooter I want to buy!" Henry says.

I have to chuckle. "It's a really cool scooter," I say. "Henry, you can do it. You can earn enough money if you keep selling drinks like you did today."

"I have a long way to go, but I think you're right," Henry says. "After today, I should be up to $80."

"The ball games are about to end," Gracie says. "What's our final count?"

I pull out all the bags. One, two, three, four . . . . I count up to 20 bags.

"We have 20 bags left," I say. "We started with 50, so that means we sold 30 bags!"

50 in total - 20 bags we have left = 30 bags sold today

I type more numbers in my calculator.

30 bags sold x $5 = $150

"The amount of money we made should be $150!" I shout.

"Really?!" Gracie says. She begins to count

the cash. I wait to hear her final count.

"Bea, we did it, we sold $150 worth!" Gracie says.

We hug each other. Our goal is to make $220 total, and we're more than half way there!

Dad drives us home. I'm so tired that I fall asleep in the car. I don't even remember dropping Gracie off at her house. I feel the car turn off, and I know we're home. I drag myself into the house, kick off my sneakers and fall into the couch. I pull a blanket up over me.

I think back over the day. I think about how worried I got about Henry's business stand—our competition.

Sometimes competition can feel kind of mean and aggressive. At other times, we need to look at competition differently. Sometimes there are ways to make the most of competition, to be flexible and to work together. Because, then, you end up doing even better than you ever thought possible.

And that's a business home run.

Chapter 10

Calling in Sick

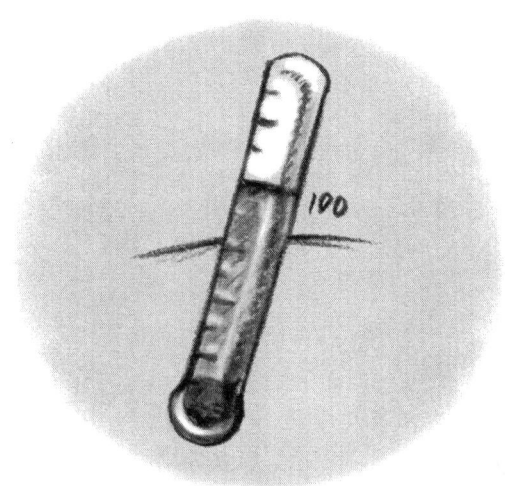

When I blink my eyes open from my nap, I know right away that it's late. I can see the sun has almost set. I can hear the hum from the television in the kitchen.

I roll over. I check my watch. It reads 8:07 p.m. Ho-ly cow. I took a three hour nap and I missed dinner altogether! The crazy thing is that I'm not even hungry. And I'm always hungry. I'm not feeling well.

"Hi sweetheart," Mom says, sitting down on the couch beside me. "Are you feeling okay?"

I groan. "I feel pretty yuck-o," I say. "My head hurts and I'm all stuffy . . . worst part is, I'm not even hungry." I turn my face into the pillow.

"Let me get you some water and we'll get you straight up to bed," Mom says.

Mom goes into the kitchen. I can hear her filling my soccer water bottle with water. I also hear her talking to Dad.

Dad comes in and scoops me up—blanket and all. He kisses me on the forehead as he carries me up the stairs. "What a bummer, kiddo. I'm sorry you're not feeling well," he says.

Mom and Dad tuck me under my covers. Hamilton curls up on his cushion at the foot of my bed. I start to drift off to sleep for the second time that evening. This time though, all I can think about is that I've got to feel better in the morning. We've GOT to sell the rest of that popcorn.

Morning comes fast.

"Mom," I say as loud as I can. *Oh, gross, my voice sounds scruffy,* I think to myself. Thank goodness Mom still hears me.

"How you feelin'?" Mom asks, peeking into the bedroom. Mom pats Hamilton as he edges his way out of my room for breakfast.

"Terrible," I say.

Mom comes and sits on the side of my bed. She feels my forehead with the back of her hand.

"You probably caught a little 24-hour bug. You'd better hang out here today," she says.

"A 24-hour bug? I don't have time for this! I wanted to go with Gracie to the ball fields again today," I sob into my pillow. It's an ugly sob.

"I totally get it," Mom says. "I'll call Gracie's mom and tell her you won't be able to make it today."

"No, Mom, I want to talk to Gracie," I say.

Mom takes out her cell phone and dials Gracie's home number. She hands me the phone when it starts to ring.

Grandma Pippa picks up.

"Hey, Grandma Pippa," I say. "It's Bea, can I talk with Gracie, please."

"Sure, honey," she says. "You feeling okay? Your voice sounds so scruffy."

"I'm sick," I say.

"Oh, gosh, I'm sorry," Grandma Pippa says. "Let me snag Gracie for you. She's on the computer right now looking up the baseball schedule."

I can hear Gracie run to the phone. I'm not looking forward to telling Gracie all this. I'm afraid it'll hurt her feelings.

"Hi ya, Bea!" Gracie says loudly.

"Hi Gracie," I say. "Hey, listen, I'm pretty sick this morning. I'm not going to be able to make it to the ball fields."

"Oh," Gracie says.

There's a long, awkward pause. It feels like the longest pause in history. I can feel her disappointment pulsing through the phone. I feel disappointed, too.

"I'm really sorry. I wish I could be there," I say. "But, listen, you can do this. I know you can."

There's another long, awkward pause.

"I don't know, Bea," Gracie says.

"Look," I say. I sit up in my bed. "Maybe

Mr. Morgan will let you make another announcement. Maybe Henry will be there again and you can set up together. Or, hey, maybe Grandma Pippa can be there, too. That'd be kind of neat since her picture is on the bags, you know?"

"Yeah," Gracie says, still disappointed.

I try to think about what might pep her up—what might help her have the confidence to take this on herself. Then, it comes to me.

I quickly do the math in my head. Since I'm not there to work, whatever Gracie sells should be hers. She'll get to keep all the money!

"Gracie, if you do as well as we did yesterday, you'll be able to reach your goal faster," I say. "Since you'll be the only person working a shift today, it's only fair that you keep all the money from today's sales. That's all cash that can go toward the Baby Blue Benedum Mixer. You could order it tonight!"

"That would mean I could have the Baby Blue Benedum Mixer by Tuesday!" Gracie says.

"You got it," I say. "Go make it happen, I know you can do it."

"I will," Gracie says. "Feel better!"

"I will," I say. I hang up the phone. I still wish I could be there. Calling in sick means passing all the responsibility to someone else. But that someone else is Gracie, and we've done enough planning to set her up to win.

Yep. Gracie is going to do just fine. In fact, she's going to do better than fine—she's going to knock it out of the park.

Chapter 11

Divvy Up

I must have taken about three long, hard naps. By the afternoon, I feel a wee bit better. I slip on my soccer sweatshirt and the warmest, fuzziest socks I can find from under my bed. I walk downstairs to the kitchen and climb onto one of the kitchen stools.

"Well hello!" I hear a voice say behind me. It's Mom.

"How are you feeling?" she asks.

"A lot better," I say. "And, guess what?"

"What?" Mom says, leaning toward me on the counter.

"I'm hungry!"

"That's a good sign," Mom smiles. "What would you like to eat?"

"Do we have any cans of Chunky Chicken Noodle Soup?" I ask.

"We sure do," Mom says, going into the pantry. "You know," she continues, "I got a text from Grandma Pippa."

"And?" I ask quickly. "How'd it go? Did she do it? Did Gracie sell everything?"

"She sure did. She sold every last one," Mom said. "Evidently the championship games were today, so there were even more people out."

"She did it!" I shout.

"They had to leave right after the seventh inning stretch because she ran out of inventory," Mom says.

"Well, that's just . . ." I pause. "AWESOME!"

Mom places the large, warm, red bowl of soup in front of me. As I sip my soup, I imagine how busy Gracie must have felt helping all those paying customers.

"I was thinking of taking Hamilton for a walk around the block," Mom says. "It's a beautiful day outside. You feel like some fresh air?"

"That sounds nice," I say. I finish slurping up my soup, shuffle down the hall and grab my 412 sneakers from the closet.

Mom and I make it several houses down the street when I see Gracie peddling toward us on her bike. She's wobbling because she's steering the bike with one hand—and waving an envelope in her other hand.

"Gracie! You did it!" I shout.

"WE did it," she says. She stops her bike right beside us.

"I've got all the cash right in here," she says. "Want to go through it? We can pay your mom back and divide out the rest."

Suddenly I feel a rush of energy. "Let's go count it up!" I say.

We walk back to my house. Gracie pushes her bicycle beside us as she tells us stories from the day. Hearing her talk about how she stepped up and owned her business today makes me kind of happy I got sick. I think Gracie needed to see she has her own superhero powers.

We settle in at the kitchen counter and separate

out all the money. We split the one dollar bills, the five dollar bills and the ten dollar bills into different piles. Then we count all the money.

$245!

"We beat our goal of $220!" I say.

"We did," Gracie confirms. "We sold $150 the first day and $95 the second day. It would have been $100 on the second day, but I split a bag of caramel popcorn with Henry and his friends."

I smile. Teamwork saved the day. Again.

I start fiddling with the money, I count up $20. I stack it neatly.

"This is what we have to pay back to my mom for the supplies," I say. "$20."

"So how much do we have left?" Gracie asks.

I type the numbers in my calculator:

$245 - $20 = $225

"We'll have $225 left over after paying my mom back for the supplies," I say.

I think about how Gracie and I should split the

money. While I'd love to have half of $225, I wasn't there on the second day. And I want to be fair.

I decide to think about it this way:

On Saturday, both of us worked a time slot, or a shift. So that makes two shifts total that day. Then on Sunday, only Gracie worked—so that's just one shift. So, two shifts on Saturday plus one shift on Sunday makes three shifts in total over the weekend.

Bea—worked 1 shift
Gracie—worked 2 shifts

"What if we split the remaining $225 dollars in three parts Gracie?" I ask. "You'll get two parts and I'll get one part since you worked two shifts and I worked one shift."

Grace nods. She's following the math in her head. "Makes sense to me."

She watches as I type in the calculation:

$225 / 3 = $75

I hold up the calculator. "It's $75 for each

shift," I say. "So I get $75, and you get $75 times two for working two shifts. That comes to $150 for you!"

Gracie looks at me with wide eyes. They're even wider than the day when I told her I'd help her with the business in the first place.

"You mean, I earned $150? That's enough to pay for my half of the Baby Blue Benedum Mixer!"

"You could buy it online tonight, Gracie," I say. I smile as I hand the $150 over to her. #Proud

Chapter 12

High-Five

Several days later, I'm in my office with Hamilton. I'm tinkering with a little pulley I bought at the hardware store with my caramel popcorn business money.

As I'm tinkering, I hear the gentle jingling of my charm bracelet. Then there's a knock at the door.

"Come in," I shout, not looking up.

"Hey, Bea!"

It's Gracie. She's holding a plate with what

looks like (and smells like!) freshly-baked cookies. She must have made them with her new Baby Blue Benedum Mixer.

"I brought these over just for you!" Gracie says.

"Really?"

"Really. I wanted to thank you for everything you did to help me."

"Oh, it was nothing, Gracie," I say.

"No, seriously, Bea. I couldn't have done it without you," she says.

As I reach for a cookie, I see Gracie looking at my bulletin board. I pinned a picture up there of me and Gracie at the baseball games. Dad snapped a photo before we were officially open for business.

I have a bunch of pictures of me and my friends on the board—and there's something all those pictures share: business.

"Bea, I think it's pretty cool that you like

business stuff as much as you do. You have a good eye for it, you know?"

"Thanks. I want to be like my mom one day. I want to run my own business, so it's kind of like practice 'til then," I say.

Gracie brushes the cookie crumbs from her fingers and works a piece of cookie from her left side jaw. She scrunches her nose. She's thinking about something.

"I heard that after every business you help launch, you set aside some money for the animal shelter," she says.

"That's true. We adopted Hamilton from that shelter, and he's my dog-brother, so I like to help them out when I can," I say. I rub Hamilton's belly as he tries to lick crumbs from my face.

"Well, I'd like you to have this." Gracie hands me an envelope. "It's not much, but I'd like to donate, too, if that's okay."

"Wow, yes, that's great," I say, nearly speechless. "Thank you, Gracie. That's really nice."

I pull out my desk drawer to find where I secretly hide a cream-colored envelope labeled 'Donations.' It's starting to tatter at the edges. I've had this envelope since my very first business venture.

"You know, I was thinking more about how lucky we are. We get to try a lot of different things and ideas that girls like Grandma Pippa or even before Grandma Pippa never got to try," says Gracie.

"We just have to believe in ourselves," I say.

"And ignore people like Nigel!" Gracie chimes in. We laugh.

"So, what's your next project?" Gracie asks.

"I'm not quite sure. But, I've got some time now, so I think I might start building the pulley system from my office to my bedroom window."

I hear my mom's voice. "Bea, Grandma Pippa is waiting for Gracie! They've got to head home now."

Gracie throws me a high-five. "Hey, guess what they're selling at lunch tomorrow?" she asks.

"Pirate Paulie's Cinnamon Pretzels?" I reply.

"You got it. Bring your sixty cents!" she says, walking out the door. "And, hey, Bea, let's talk tomorrow about some ideas on how I could start selling these cookies now."

"You got it!" I reply. Gracie waves and runs back to the house.

I'm sitting in the office with Hamilton. I look at the picture of me and Gracie at the baseball fields.

I am pretty lucky to get these chances to start businesses with my friends. And to practice believing in, well . . . me, I think to myself.

I pull the Andrew Carnegie quote off my bulletin board. I hold it up and read it.

Think of yourself as on the threshold of unparalleled success. A whole, clear, glorious life lies before you. Achieve! Achieve!

Grandma Pippa said how lucky we are to have so many opportunities. What will I do when I'm bigger? What opportunities will come my way? Will I keep doing businesses? Will I do something bigger and better than I can even imagine?

I look at my hand as it holds the Andrew Carnegie card. My hot Pinks-burgh nail polish has nearly all chipped off. It's been a busy week. I'm tapping the toe of my left shoe.

"Come on Hamilton, let's go inside," I say. "I've got an idea." I shut the office door, hide the key in the planter box, and I tighten the laces on my 412 sneakers. We take off running toward the house.

Chapter 13

Your Project!

BUSINESS OF THE DAY: A Tasty Tally Up!

Want to try taste testing caramel popcorn, just like Bea? You can! Simply join a parent or grandparent on a trip to the grocery store and purchase two different bags of caramel popcorn. Then, make a survey to get feedback from your family and friends to find out which popcorn they prefer!

WHY YOU'RE DOING THIS:

- Learn about the process of making and using a survey.
- See why a survey is a good way to learn about a topic or a product.
- Have fun with business in a different way!

TODAY'S AGENDA:

Step 1: Buy two different bags of caramel popcorn

Step 2: Make your surveys

Step 3: Conduct your survey research

Step 4: Tally up your results

Let's get started!

Step 1: Buy two different bags of caramel popcorn

Head to the grocery store with a parent or grandparent and buy two bags of caramel popcorn.

Try to find two different brands of the same flavor of caramel popcorn. For example, make sure they both either have nuts or don't have nuts—that will make sure you're comparing two similar products.

> **TIP:** If you have some money saved up in a piggy bank, why not offer to pay for the bags all by yourself!? That's a good business practice.

Step 2: Make your surveys

Type up your survey on the computer. You may use the one provided in this section if you want—or change it to ask other questions that YOU think of on your own. The survey on the next page is an A and B survey, so it asks your taste testers to choose between two items—in this case, your two caramel popcorn brands—when asked different questions.

Print out however many copies you'll need. This depends on how many people will be taste testing. So, if you have four taste testers, print out four survey copies.

Survey

Type and print out this set of survey questions below (or use your own questions!) See if you can get three or more people to try the popcorn and fill out a survey. If you don't have a printer, just get writing! In business, there's always a way.

Ask each person to answer the survey questions below:
Which popcorn has a better buttery taste? **A or B**
Which popcorn has a better caramel flavor? **A or B**
Which popcorn has a better crunchy texture? **A or B**
Which popcorn has a better salty flavor? **A or B**
Which popcorn has a better sweet flavor? **A or B**
Which popcorn do you like better overall? **A or B**

[Add any other questions you think of here.]

Step 3: Conduct your survey research

You've purchased your popcorn and your surveys are ready. Now it's time to put the caramel popcorn into two separate bowls. Label one bowl "Bowl A" and label the second bowl "Bowl B." Something like this:

In secret, write on a piece of paper which bag you bought is in the "Bowl A" bowl and which bag is in the "Bowl B" bowl.

Once your taste testers try the two types of caramel popcorn and finish their surveys, gather all your surveys in a pile.

Step 4: Tally up your results

Now it's time to tally up your results!

To tally up, grab a piece of scratch paper. Make one column for Bowl A and one column for Bowl B. Any time someone chose Bowl A in their survey questions, make a notch in column A. Any time someone chose Bowl B in their survey, make a notch in column B.

Which one of the caramel popcorn bags got more points? That is the one your taste testers preferred. Now, you can take a break and enjoy the popcorn with your family and friends!

~ KEEP LEARNING ABOUT BUSINESS ~

For more educational resources or to consult with Bea on your child's business idea, please visit us at www.beaisforbusiness.com, follow us on Twitter (@bea4biz) or like us on Facebook (www.facebook.com/bea4biz)!

THE FAMILY CONFERENCE CALL:
Questions to Talk About Together

- Can you think of a time when you've seen a survey? What was it for?
- Why would a company make a survey? What kinds of things would they be trying to find out?
- What was your favorite part of the "Tasty Tally Up" project?
- Which popcorn won and was it the one you preferred?
- Why do you think people preferred the one popcorn over the other?
- Why are surveys helpful in learning about a topic or a product?

Made in the USA
San Bernardino, CA
20 November 2014